ADVANCING
FORMATIVE
ASSESSMENT
IN EVERY CLASSROOM

a GUIDE FOR INSTRUCTIONAL LEADERS

ASCD MEMBER BOOK

Many ASCD members received this book as a
member benefit upon its initial release.

Learn more at: **www.ascd.org/memberbooks**

ASCD cares about Planet Earth.
This book has been printed on environmentally friendly paper.

ADVANCING
FORMATIVE ASSESSMENT
IN EVERY CLASSROOM

a GUIDE FOR INSTRUCTIONAL LeaDERS

CONNIE M. MOSS
SUSAN M. BROOKHART

ASCD | Alexandria, Virginia

1703 N. Beauregard St. • Alexandria, VA 22311-1714 USA
Phone: 800-933-2723 or 703-578-9600 • Fax: 703-575-5400
Web site: www.ascd.org • E-mail: member@ascd.org
Author guidelines: www.ascd.org/write

Gene R. Carter, *Executive Director;* Nancy Modrak, *Publisher;* Scott Willis, *Director, Book Acquisitions & Development;* Genny Ostertag, *Content Development;* Julie Houtz, *Director, Book Editing & Production;* Miriam Goldstein, *Editor;* Sima Jaafar, *Senior Graphic Designer;* Mike Kalyan, *Production Manager;* Cynthia Stock, *Typesetter;* Sarah Plumb, *Production Specialist*

Printed in the United States of America. Cover art © 2009 by ASCD. ASCD publications present a variety of viewpoints. The views expressed or implied in this book should not be interpreted as official positions of the Association.

All Web links in this book are correct as of the publication date below but may have become inactive or otherwise modified since that time. If you notice a deactivated or changed link, please e-mail books@ascd.org with the words "Link Update" in the subject line. In your message, please specify the Web link, the book title, and the page number on which the link appears.

ASCD Member Book, No. FY10-3 (Dec. 2009, P). ASCD Member Books mail to Premium (P), Select (S), and Institutional Plus (I+) members on this schedule: Jan., PSI+; Feb., P; Apr., PSI+; May, P; July, PSI+; Aug., P; Sept., PSI+; Nov., PSI+; Dec., P. Select membership was formerly known as Comprehensive membership.

PAPERBACK ISBN: 978-1-4166-0911-7   ASCD product #109031

Also available as an e-book (see Books in Print for the ISBNs).

Quantity discounts for the paperback edition only: 10–49 copies, 10%; 50+ copies, 15%; for 1,000 or more copies, call 800-933-2723, ext. 5634, or 703-575-5634. For desk copies: member@ascd.org.

Library of Congress Cataloging-in-Publication Data

Moss, Connie M.
    Advancing formative assessment in every classroom: a guide for instructional leaders / Connie M. Moss and Susan M. Brookhart.
        p. cm.
    Includes bibliographical references and index.
    ISBN 978-1-4166-0911-7 (pbk. : alk. paper)
    1. Teachers—In-service training. 2. Educational evaluation—United States. 3. Group work in education—United States. I. Brookhart, Susan M. II. Title.
    LB1731.M66 2009
    371.26'4—dc22
                                                                                            2009032467

20 19 18 17 16 15 14 13 12 11 10 09   1 2 3 4 5 6 7 8 9 10 11 12

ADVANCING
FORMative
ASSESSMENT
IN EVERY CLASSROOM

a Guide For INSTRUCTIONAL LeaDers

acknowledgments

We are fortunate to work with educators and students who are a constant source of ideas and encouragement. This book would not be the same without you.

We are particularly privileged to partner with the teachers, administrators, and students in the Armstrong School District in Pennsylvania as they work to intentionally advance formative assessment in classrooms. We especially thank Dr. Beverly Long, our colleague and friend, for her leadership.

We acknowledge the contributions of our talented colleagues and friends at the Center for Advancing the Study of Teaching and Learning in the Duquesne University School of Education: David Goldbach, Amy Protos, Susan Bianco, and Rick McCown.

And finally, we extend our deepest gratitude to our families:

Connie thanks her husband John and family—Rita, Clara, Mary Jo, Fred, and Rosemarie—for their faith in her and for always being there. And most of all, she thanks her daughter Rachael and her late father Alfred for their courage and inspiration.

Sue thanks her family—Frank, Carol, and Rachel—for their love and support.

INTRODUCTION

Formative assessment, when used effectively, can significantly improve student achievement and raise teacher quality. Yet high-quality formative assessment is rarely a consistent part of the classroom culture. Teachers are neither sufficiently familiar with it nor equipped with the knowledge or the skill to put formative assessment to work for themselves and their students.

This book is intended as a resource for school leaders as they work with teachers to make the formative assessment process an integral part of their classrooms. We focus on classroom-level practices that affect student learning and achievement, build capacity, and foster schoolwide outcomes that can meet the demands for high-stakes accountability facing today's education professionals. And amid calls for data-driven decision making, we intentionally focus the book on practices that put information about learning into the hands of the most important decision makers of all—the students.

We have organized this book so that school leaders, school teams, and collaborative groups can use it as a guide to engage in highly effective formative assessment practices that promote school improvement and increase student achievement. We place particular emphasis on the ways that the formative assessment process enables students to harness the workings of their own minds to become intentional and skilled learners.

We begin in Chapter 1 with an overview of the formative assessment process—what it is and what it is not. Then, to emphasize classroom practices that not only help students achieve but also help them learn how to learn, we have organized the next six chapters around six elements of the formative assessment process—one per chapter—that we believe have a particularly powerful effect on student learning and teacher quality. We have arranged the elements in a logical sequence that has been, in our experience, very successful in helping teachers integrate formative assessment practices in ways that build on the elements' interrelated nature to maximize their effect. School leaders who support and coach teachers in these practices will help teachers and students succeed. We use the following set of Q&A prompts to examine each element of the process and show its connection to increased student achievement and motivation to learn:

- What is it?
- How does it affect student learning and achievement?
- What common misconceptions might teachers hold?
- What is the "motivation connection"?
- What are specific strategies I can share with teachers?
- How will I recognize it when I see it?
- How can I model it in conversations with teachers about their own professional learning?
- What if?

As the sequence of questions suggests, we structure each chapter first to "tell." We explain the element of the formative assessment process, supporting our description with relevant research on its effects in the classroom. Next, we use classroom examples to "show" how teachers and their students can incorporate formative assessment into their day-to-day, minute-by-minute teaching and learning. Finally, we suggest strategies for using highly effective classroom practices that boost student achievement, maximize the collection and use of strong evidence of student learning, and bring increased clarity and coherence to the teaching-learning process. These strategies are useful for all teachers in all grades, subjects, and content areas. In other words, each of these chapters not only covers the "what" and the "how" but also begins with perhaps the most important aspect, the "why."

We also use Chapters 2 through 7 to describe practical ways that school leaders can model and use the elements of the formative assessment process during conversations with teachers. We envision these conversations happening as part of formal classroom observations and informal classroom walk-throughs and during other communication with individual teachers and teacher groups. These formative conversations can enrich professional relationships, promote a schoolwide culture of inquiry, and encourage teachers to learn together about the significant relationship that exists between the quality of their teaching practices and the level of student achievement in their classrooms.

We finish each of these chapters by providing two ways for educational leaders to extend their thinking about the focus of the chapter. First, we provide a short "What If?" scenario to help you think through possible challenges and to offer supportive advice. Second, we suggest reflection questions to assist you in gauging where you are in terms of high-quality formative assessment practices. Finally, each chapter concludes with a summary of the major points.

In the book's final chapter, we discuss taking formative assessment schoolwide and note the role that formative assessment can play in transforming all learning and all learners in the school. As educators inquire together about the quality of their classroom practices, they can continually refine their professional knowledge and expertise.

It is our hope that the ideas presented here will lead to increased understanding of how formative assessment can affect student learning and achievement, because after all is said and done, that is its primary purpose. We also hope that school leaders will see this book as a resource they can tap again and again as they use the formative assessment process to dramatically influence teaching and learning in their schools.

1

THE LAY OF THE LAND:
Essential Elements of the Formative Assessment Process

When teachers join forces with their students in the formative assessment process, their partnership generates powerful learning outcomes. Teachers become more effective, students become actively engaged, and they both become intentional learners.

We can use the metaphor of a windmill to visualize the formative assessment process and its effects. Just as a windmill intentionally harnesses the power of moving air to generate energy, the formative assessment process helps students intentionally harness the workings of their own minds to generate motivation to learn. Propelled by the formative assessment process, students understand and use learning targets, set their own learning goals, select effective learning strategies, and assess their own learning progress. And as students develop into more confident and competent learners, they become motivated (energized) to learn, increasingly able to persist during demanding tasks and to regulate their own effort and actions when they tackle new learning challenges.

When a windmill whirls into action, its individual blades seem to disappear. The same thing happens to the six elements of the formative assessment process. These interrelated elements are the following:

- Shared learning targets and criteria for success
- Feedback that feeds forward

- Student goal setting
- Student self-assessment
- Strategic teacher questioning
- Student engagement in asking effective questions

As teachers and students actively and intentionally engage in learning, the individual elements unite in a flurry of cognitive activity, working together and depending on each other. Their power comes from their combined effort.

What Is Formative Assessment?

Formative assessment is an active and intentional learning process that partners the teacher and the students to continuously and systematically gather evidence of learning with the express goal of improving student achievement. Intentional learning refers to cognitive processes that have learning as a goal rather than an incidental outcome (Bereiter & Scardamalia, 1989). Teachers and their students actively and intentionally engage in the formative assessment process when they work together to do the following (Brookhart, 2006):

- Focus on learning goals.
- Take stock of where current work is in relation to the goal.
- Take action to move closer to the goal.

The primary purpose of formative assessment is to improve learning, not merely to audit it. It is assessment *for* learning rather than assessment *of* learning. Formative assessment is both an "instructional tool" that teachers and their students "use while learning is occurring" and "an accountability tool to determine if learning has occurred" (National Education Association, 2003, p. 3). In other words, to be "formative," assessments must inform the decisions that teachers and their students make minute by minute in the classroom. Figure 1.1 compares the characteristics of formative assessment and summative assessment.

Here are some examples of the formative assessment process in the classroom:

- A teacher asks students in his 6th grade social studies class to form pairs to generate three strategic questions that will help them better meet their learning target of describing how erosion has produced physical patterns on the earth's surface that have affected human activities.

FIGURE 1.1
Characteristics of Formative and Summative Assessment

Formative Assessment (Assessment *for* Learning)	Summative Assessment (Assessment *of* Learning)
Purpose: To improve learning and achievement	**Purpose:** To measure or audit attainment
Carried out while learning is in progress—day to day, minute by minute.	Carried out from time to time to create snapshots of what has happened.
Focused on the learning process and the learning progress.	Focused on the products of learning.
Viewed as an integral part of the teaching-learning process.	Viewed as something separate, an activity performed after the teaching-learning cycle.
Collaborative—Teachers and students know where they are headed, understand the learning needs, and use assessment information as feedback to guide and adapt what they do to meet those needs.	*Teacher directed*—Teachers assign what the students must do and then evaluate how well they complete the assignment.
Fluid—An ongoing process influenced by student need and teacher feedback.	*Rigid*—An unchanging measure of what the student achieved.
Teachers and students adopt the role of intentional learners.	Teachers adopt the role of auditors and students assume the role of the audited.
Teachers and students use the evidence they gather to make adjustments for continuous improvement.	Teachers use the results to make final "success or failure" decisions about a relatively fixed set of instructional activities.

- Before a lesson on creating a family budget, a consumer science teacher states the goals for the lesson and asks the students to paraphrase the goals.
- In a high school English class, students use a rubric that they generated as a class to plan their essays, monitor their writing, and edit their drafts in order to meet the criteria for a successful essay.

- In his feedback to a 1st grade student, a teacher shows the student what she did correctly in her attempt to draw the life cycle of a frog. Then the teacher gives the student a strategy to use to improve the accuracy of her drawing before she turns in her final sketch.
- A middle school student decides to use a story map to plan his short story depicting life in the Victorian era. It will help him reach his goal of improving the organization and sequencing of his story.

What Three Questions Guide the Formative Assessment Process?

The formative assessment process aligns what happens in the classroom—day to day and minute by minute—with three central questions:

- Where am I going?
- Where am I now?
- What strategy or strategies can help me get to where I need to go?

These central questions guide everything the teacher does, everything the student does, and everything teachers and their students do together. The questions are deceptively simple, yet to address them students and teachers must become skilled assessors who can gauge the gap between the students' current level of understanding and the shared learning target. Only then can they choose appropriate strategies to close the gap.

This continuous process of setting a learning target, assessing present levels of understanding, and then working strategically to narrow the distance between the two is the essence of formative assessment. Once a learning target is mastered, a new "just right" target is set and the process continues forward. It comes down to the Goldilocks Principle: to generate motivation to learn, the level of challenge and the level of support must be just right. And that means all classroom decisions—those made by the teacher and those made by the students themselves—must be informed by continually gathering evidence of student learning.

The three central questions of the formative assessment process are a great starting point for school leaders as they help teachers recognize and use formative assessment in their classrooms. The questions can guide teachers as they (1) plan their lessons, (2) monitor their teaching, and (3) help their students become self-regulated learners. Teachers can display the questions in their classrooms and remind their students to think about them before, during, and after each learning experience.

How Does the Formative Assessment Process Affect Student Learning and Achievement?

> There is a firm body of evidence that formative assessment is an essential component of classroom work and that its development can raise standards of achievement. We know of no other way of raising standards for which such a strong prima facie case can be made.
>
> —Paul Black & Dylan Wiliam,
> "Inside the Black Box: Raising Standards Through Classroom Assessment"

The research is clear: formative assessment works. It works because it has a direct effect on the two most important players in the teaching-learning process: the teacher and the student.

In too many classrooms, teachers and their students are flying blind. Teachers cannot point to strong evidence of exactly what their students know and exactly where their students are in relation to daily classroom learning goals. The lack of detailed and current evidence makes it particularly difficult for teachers to provide effective feedback that describes for students the next steps they should take to improve. Students are operating in the dark as well. Without the benefit of knowing how to assess and regulate their own learning, they try to perform well on assignments without knowing exactly where they are headed, what they need to do to get there, and how they will tell when they have arrived.

Effects on Teacher Quality

Teacher quality exerts greater influence on student achievement than any other factor in education—no other factor even comes close (Darling-Hammond, 1999; Hanushek, Kain, O'Brien, & Rivkin, 2005; Thompson & Wiliam, 2007). Formative assessment affects teacher quality because it operates at the core of effective teaching (Black & Wiliam, 1998; Elmore, 2004). Engaged in the formative assessment process, teachers learn about effective teaching by studying the effectiveness of their own instructional decisions. This practice promotes professional learning that is relevant, authentic, and transformational.

Despite professional development efforts focused on training teachers to use best practices in their classroom, studies clearly show that teachers do not always teach in ways that research supports as best practices for student learning. Rather, teachers teach in ways they *believe* to be best, often ignoring the findings of educational research. The distinction here is critical. Teachers' beliefs not only determine what they do in the classroom but also influence what they count as evidence that learning has occurred. And unless professional learning experiences help teachers examine their working assumptions about how students learn and how good teaching supports learning, they will not make meaningful changes in their teaching practices (Moss, 2002; Schreiber, Moss, & Staab, 2007).

Formative assessment can have a transformational effect on teachers and teaching (see Figure 1.2). In a very real way it flips a switch, shining a bright light on individual teaching decisions so that teachers can see clearly (and perhaps for the first time) the difference between the *intent* and the *effect* of their actions. Armed with this new perspective, teachers can take constructive action in their classrooms. They begin to collect and use strong evidence of exactly what works and exactly what does not work in their classrooms, with their students. And as they critically examine their own knowledge, practices, and working assumptions—during each day, during each lesson, and during each interaction with their students—they become inquiry-minded and keenly aware of exactly where they need to focus their change and improvement efforts in order to raise student achievement.

Effects on Student Learning

The effects of the formative assessment process on students are just as dramatic because it engages students in learning how to learn. Students learn more, learn smarter, and grow into self-aware learners who can tell you exactly what they did to get to exactly where they are. In other words, students become self-regulated learners and data-driven decision makers. They learn to gather evidence about their own learning and to use that information to choose from a growing collection of strategies for success. And students not only learn how to take

FIGURE 1.2

Impact of the Formative Assessment Process on Teachers

Teachers Adopt a Working Assumption That . . .	Teachers Take Constructive Action to . . .
Students learn more effectively when they know and understand the learning goal.	• Bring precision to their planning. • Communicate learning goals in student-friendly language. • Unpack the exact criteria students must meet to succeed on each task.
To help each student succeed, I must know precisely where that student is in relation to the learning goal.	• Continuously collect evidence of student learning to monitor and adapt their teaching during a lesson.
Effective feedback provides specific suggestions for closing the gap between where students are and where they need to be in relation to the learning goal.	• Give feedback that is focused, generative, and descriptive. • Develop a repertoire of feedback strategies.
One of the most important skills I can teach my students is how to regulate their own learning.	• Teach their students how to self-assess. • Make rubrics, checklists, guides, and other metacognitive tools an integral part of what students do before, during, and after learning.
Meaningful learning happens between minds, during strategic conversations, and when students become models of success for each other.	• Encourage students to become learning resources for each other. • Plan for and ask strategic questions that will produce evidence of student learning.
Motivation isn't something I can give to my students; it is something I must help them develop.	• Align appropriate levels of challenge and just-right support. • Intentionally create learning experiences in which students learn what they do well, what they should do more of, and how to focus their efforts to maximize success.

ownership of their learning but also increasingly view themselves as autonomous, confident, and capable.

This combination of learning factors—ownership, autonomy, confidence, and capability—fortifies students with increased levels of resilience. Raising student resilience can derail a dangerous cycle for many students who attribute their failure to perform well on classroom tasks to a lack of academic ability. Judging themselves to be incapable of achieving and powerless to change things, they become discouraged and quit trying (Ames, 1992; Boston, 2002; Vispoel & Austin, 1995). Resilient learners, on the other hand, bounce back from poor performances and adversities. They attribute their failures and their successes on learning tasks to factors *within* their control. They rebound rather than giving up in the face of a challenge. Resilient students believe in their capacity to adapt what they are doing and how they are doing it in order to succeed.

And although formative assessment has a significant effect on learning for all students, it "helps low achievers more than other students and so reduces the range of achievement while raising achievement overall" (Black & Wiliam, 1998). For reasons we mention here and for many more we explore in later chapters, the formative assessment process is a compelling force for increasing student learning and closing the achievement gap.

How Does Formative Assessment Forge a Teacher-Student Learning Partnership?

High-quality formative assessment blurs the artificial barriers between teaching, learning, and assessment to forge a culture of collaborative inquiry and improvement in the classroom. As this learning partnership grows stronger, conversations about learning become the rule of thumb rather than the exception to the rule. Teachers and students work together to gather information about the strengths and weaknesses of their performances in ways that inform *all* learners and *all* learning in the classroom. They do this by talking with one another, planning with one another, comparing evidence of learning, and setting shared learning goals that establish the parameters of what counts as evidence that learning has indeed occurred.

The bottom line is that formative assessment fundamentally changes the quality and quantity of teacher-student interactions. And every day, throughout the day, what happens in the classroom focuses squarely on student achievement.

What Common Misconceptions Might Teachers Hold About Formative Assessment?

Misconceptions are the inevitable result of misunderstanding and often cause teachers to question the formative assessment process. Clearly these misconceptions can dilute the effectiveness of formative assessment and block its consistent use in the classroom. School leaders can take an active role in helping teachers build accurate understandings of what formative assessment is and, perhaps most important, what it *is not*. They can include strategic talking points in their initial and ongoing conversations with teachers about formative assessment. Here we identify common misconceptions and suggest strategic talking points for each.

Misconception #1: Formative assessment is a special kind of test or series of tests that teachers learn to use to find out what their students know. This is probably the most common misconception regarding formative assessment. It is directly related to our sometimes careless custom of using the terms *assessment* and *test* interchangeably. Is it any wonder teachers mistakenly assume that formative assessment is a special kind of test item, test, or series of tests—something that they must administer *to* their students in order to audit learning?

Strategic talking points school leaders can use to address this misconception include the following:

- Formative assessment is not a test item, a test, or a series of tests.
- Formative assessment is an intentional learning process teachers engage in *with* their students to gather information *during* the learning process to improve achievement.
- Formative assessment is a learning partnership that involves teachers and their students taking stock of where they are in relation to their learning goals.

Misconception #2: Formative assessment is a program that teachers adopt and add to what they already do. This misconception can be traced directly to traditional inservice workshop models of professional development. More times than not, teachers are asked to enact a program or technique prescribed by outside experts and presented to them in a one-shot workshop. It stands to reason, then, that teachers often view formative assessment as a program or method they must learn and add to what they already do. This misguided view often leads teachers to wonder how they will find time to "do formative assessment" along with everything else they already "do" in their classrooms. This additive perspective makes it particularly difficult for teachers to recognize formative assessment as a dynamic process that shifts the classroom focus from instruction to learning and represents much more than simply adding a new technique to what currently exists.

Strategic talking points school leaders can use to address this misconception include the following:

- Formative assessment is not a prepackaged program or set of techniques that teachers adopt and enact.
- Formative assessment is a philosophy of teaching and learning in which the purpose of assessing is to inform learning, not merely to audit it.
- The formative assessment process is a fundamental reframing of the work teachers and students do day to day and minute by minute in the classroom.

Misconception #3: Any practice that gathers information for the purpose of improving programs or improving teaching is a part of formative assessment. The final misconception lies at the core of what qualifies a practice as formative assessment. Some educators mistakenly conclude that when teachers use assessment information to redesign or change a lesson, they meet the criteria of formative assessment. For example, a high school history teacher notes a troubling pattern on the final exam for her World War II unit. Half of her students mistakenly identified Germany as the country that suffered the most lasting damage from the war. As a result, she plans to change the way she teaches that content to her students next year. She intends to spend more time discussing the concept of lasting damage so that her future students can draw conclusions that are more accurate. In this example, the teacher uses information gathered after instruction to plan improved learning experiences for future students. Although the teacher's plan is laudable, it is not an example of formative assessment.

Strategic talking points school leaders can use to address this misconception include the following:

- To be considered part of the formative assessment process, information gathered must be used to inform the learning of *current* students.
- Although the quality of teaching rises as a result of formative assessment, the intended outcome must be to raise the learning and achievement of the students currently in the classroom on the concepts, processes, and skills that formed the basis for the assessment.

What Is the Connection Between Formative Assessment and Motivation?

The term *motivation* comes from the root word *motive*, which means "something that causes a person to act." Using that root, we can define motivation as something that energizes, directs, and sustains behavior toward a goal. Another way to say this is that motivation is goal-directed behavior combined with the energy and the intention to work toward that goal. In a very real way, motivation gets students learning, points them in the right direction, and keeps them engaged.

Although teachers cannot "give" motivation to their students, they can nurture, foster, and help their students develop more of it. Many educators view motivation as something that comes from external factors such as rewards, incentives, punishments, and warnings—carrots and sticks. This view is not exactly flawed, because one form of motivation, extrinsic motivation, fits nicely into this description. The crux of the matter, though, is that extrinsic motivation applied to the classroom requires that the teacher use rewards (such as stickers, grades, free time, bonus points) and punishments (such as loss of recess, detention, lowering a grade) to control the motivation of students. It follows that students will only be motivated as long as they are under the control of the teacher. Without the teacher, the motivation disappears. So much for lifelong learning!

In fact, research tells us that extrinsic rewards can actually undermine a student's internal (intrinsic) motivation over time. The most detrimental practices involve giving rewards as a direct function of a student's performance. These rewards follow a common pattern. Students who perform the best get the most rewards, and those who perform less well get fewer or no rewards. For students who cannot meet the requirements, this type of external control chips away at them over time to weaken their motivation to learn, undercut their performance, and leave them demoralized (Deci, Koestner, & Ryan, 1999). Understanding this effect, then, teachers should use extrinsic rewards sparingly and *always* as part of a plan to activate intrinsic motivation so that the external rewards can be gradually decreased and eventually removed.

In contrast, the formative assessment process has no downside. In fact, it is strongly linked to increased intrinsic student motivation. Like the windmill, formative assessment helps students harness the workings of their own minds to continuously generate and strengthen these four important components of motivation to learn:

- Self-efficacy—A learner's belief in his ability to succeed in a particular situation
- Self-regulation—The degree to which a learner is metacognitively, motivationally, and actively participating in her own learning
- Self-assessment—A learner's act of observing, analyzing, and judging his own performance on the basis of criteria and determining how he can improve it
- Self-attribution—A learner's own perceptions or explanations for success or failure that determine the amount of effort she will expend on that activity in the future

Throughout the remaining chapters, we will further unpack what we call the "motivation connection" by examining how the specific elements of the formative assessment process link to the components of intrinsic motivation. Figure 1.3 highlights those links and previews our upcoming examinations of the power of the formative assessment process to generate motivation to learn.

FIGURE 1.3
Links Between Formative Assessment and Intrinsic Motivation

Formative Assessment Elements . . .	. . . Help Students Harness the Workings of Their Own Minds in the Following Ways . . .	. . . to Generate Components of Motivation to Learn
Shared Learning Targets and Criteria for Success	• Directs students and teachers toward specific goals. • Increases initiation for the learning task. • Helps students and teachers monitor learning progress.	
Feedback That Feeds Forward	• Enhances cognitive processing. • Fosters resiliency and persistence in the face of challenge. • Provides students with specific next-step strategies.	
Student Goal Setting	• Increases active student engagement. • Shifts student focus from performance-directed to goal-directed behavior. • Induces effort, increases persistence, and promotes development of new strategies.	• Self-efficacy • Self-assessment • Self-regulation • Self-attribution
Student Self-Assessment	• Shifts power from the teacher to the student. • Engages students in actively collecting and interpreting assessment information. • Helps students set more realistic and active goals for continuously raising achievement.	
Strategic Teacher Questioning	• Directs students and teachers toward salient elements of the content, process, or performance. • Scaffolds learners as they move beyond partial, thin, or passive understandings. • Promotes conceptual change.	
Engagement of Students in Asking Effective Questions	• Increases intentional and active student engagement. • Promotes autonomy and independence. • Develops students' perceptions of themselves as producers of knowledge and generators of important lines of inquiry. • Gives students confidence to work through difficulties themselves.	

How Will I Recognize the Formative Assessment Process When I See It?

Because formative assessment is a systematic and intentional process of gathering evidence of learning, you can observe its effects in the classroom. These effects include what the teacher does, what the students do, what the products and performances look like, and how teachers talk about their students' learning. Figure 1.4 shows some examples of what you can look for inside the classroom. In upcoming chapters we share more "look fors" as we examine the specific elements of the formative assessment process.

How Can I Model the Formative Assessment Process in Conversations with Teachers About Their Own Professional Learning?

The formative assessment process constantly uses evidence to guide teaching and learning. When school leaders enter into collaborative inquiry with teachers, they not only model the formative assessment process, they embody it. Research on professional development tells us that when principals engage in periodic, short, focused, individual conversations with a teacher, they advance professional learning and produce positive change in teacher behavior in ways that far surpass the effects of the traditional "sit and get" workshops (Hall & Hord, 2000). In fact, one of the most strategic actions school leaders can take to bring about increased student achievement is to center their efforts directly on the inner workings of the classroom (Elmore, 2000).

School leaders can use formative discussions with teachers to promote "systematic and intentional inquiry" (Moss, 2000; Moss & McCown, 2007) into their classroom practices. Formative assessment operates at the nexus of what teachers believe to be true about teaching and learning, how those beliefs shape the ways teachers choose to teach, and the effects of instructional decisions on student achievement and motivation to learn. Each element of the formative assessment process helps educators assess what they are doing in their classrooms, why they are doing it, and how their choices are affecting their students. And because the formative assessment process requires teachers to use information

FIGURE 1.4

Recognizing the Formative Assessment Process

Formative Assessment: An active and intentional learning process that partners the teacher and the students to continuously and systematically gather evidence of learning with the express goal of improving student achievement.

Teacher "Look Fors"	Student "Look Fors"
Teachers . . .	Students . . .
• Share learning goals in developmentally appropriate ways.	• Understand and can explain what they do well and exactly what they should do next.
• Adjust their teaching on the fly to deepen student understanding and clear up misconceptions.	• Recognize when they are learning and when they are not.
• Plan the questions they will ask throughout the lesson to help students focus on salient aspects of important concepts and the criteria for a successful performance.	• Use teacher-made rubrics, checklists, and guides to monitor and adjust the quality of their learning performance.
• Teach specific metacognitive strategies to maximize student success.	• Can adapt their learning strategies to meet their learning needs.
• Provide feedback that is clear, descriptive, and task specific, and show students where they are in relation to the goal and what they should do next to close the gap.	• Set their own learning goals and monitor their progress.
• Greet student questions with respect and enthusiasm and respond in thoughtful ways.	• Can assess their own work or performance in relation to the criteria for success.
• Use provocative questions to prompt student reflection on their understanding and performance.	• Set realistic short-term goals for where they want to be, the strategy they will use to get there, and the criteria they will apply to determine they have succeeded.
• Model self-assessment using the kinds of reasoning skills that students will use to succeed at the task at hand.	• Ask questions that seek clarity concerning concepts, tasks, and reasoning processes.
• Describe student learning along a continuum of progress toward a specific learning goal, noting plans for adjusting instruction and levels of support to promote student growth.	• Appear confident, engaged, and motivated to learn.
	• Describe their learning in terms of where they are in relation to the learning goal and what they intend to do next to keep making progress.

about student learning to guide and promote student achievement, it helps their instructional decisions become increasingly intentional and scientifically based. The ability of formative assessment to promote and sustain active teacher inquiry that is both systematic and intentional is exactly why it can have a significant effect on daily classroom practices. Simply put, formative assessment situates powerful professional learning in the heartbeat of the classroom and encourages educators to approach their teaching as "intentional learning" (Moss, 2001).

As schools become places of collaborative inquiry, school leaders can use formative discussions to take a collegial rather than a supervisory perspective on professional learning, focus on each teacher's unique expertise and professional learning needs, and promote teacher collaboration to improve instruction (Glickman, Gordon, & Ross-Gordon, 1998). School leaders can use well-chosen starter statements that encourage shared inquiry. These starter statements situate the interaction as a formative conversation, center it on professional self-analysis of patterns of practice rather than ramifications of particular incidents, and keep the dialogue free from judgment or evaluation. The statements signal that the teacher is in charge of his or her own professional learning and indicate interest and support. These formative conversations can preview or follow a scheduled classroom visit with a single teacher. In addition, they can serve or launch collaborative inquiry among individuals in a small group or an entire school.

Strategic conversation starters signal that teachers are in charge of their own professional learning and indicate your interest and support. Here are some examples of how to begin a formative conversation with an individual teacher:

- *I know you pride yourself on reaching and teaching all students. I'd like to spend some time thinking with you about ways to collect strong evidence that students are achieving.*
- *I wanted to catch up and talk with you more about strategies you are using to increase student goal setting and self-assessment.*
- *The last time we talked you were concerned that your students were not skilled at regulating their own learning and you planned to use rubrics to help them become more competent in that area. Talk with me a bit about your students' self-regulation progress.*

Here are some examples of how you might begin a formative conversation with a group:

- *We are acutely aware of the need for our students to improve their reading abilities. Think with me about strategies we can all commit to using and monitoring that will increase the quality of reading for understanding across grade levels and the curriculum. In our conversations, let's be sure that these strategies meet the criteria for formative assessment.*
- *During my classroom walk-throughs this week, I want to focus on the ways we are integrating formative assessment into our daily classroom practice. Think with me about a focus question that would guide the walk-throughs and our lesson planning for the week.*
- *It looks like we are making great progress in our efforts to provide effective feedback to our students. Let's keep that focus in the mix as we discuss how we can continuously and systematically improve the quality of our student feedback by sharing the feedback strategies that work best for each of us and the evidence that we gather to increase our confidence in these strategies.*

Notice that all of the examples open with an invitation to the teachers to think with you. The examples begin a conversation about teaching rather than signal an interrogation. Interrogating can trigger unwanted emotional baggage, derail collaborative inquiry efforts, be interpreted as confrontational, and signal that a grilling is waiting in the wings (Downey, Steffy, English, Frase, & Poston, 2004).

What If?

Given the realities of schools and schooling, there is a good chance teachers are already dealing with a variety of initiatives to improve teaching and learning and may be confused about how formative assessment is distinguished from other forms of assessment or data gathering. *What if you overhear a conversation among a group of teachers about how they feel benchmark assessments are the same as formative assessment?*

The first point to use to address this misconception is that benchmark assessments are interim assessments—they take place periodically, and although they are important for gauging student learning relative to content standards at a particular point in time, they do not inform teachers and students minute by minute during the learning process. Formative assessment, on the other hand, is a learning process and a learning partnership. Formative assessment provides students and teachers with the information needed to adjust teaching and learning while they are happening. And although benchmark assessments can tell teachers where students are in relation to the benchmark, the formative assessment process helps both teachers *and* students gauge student understanding all along the way.

Second, focus the teachers' attention on how the information from benchmark assessments is used compared with how formative assessment informs learning in real time—day to day and minute by minute in the classroom. Do benchmark assessments inform the learning for *current* students with the current learning target?

And, perhaps most important, help teachers see that benchmark assessments do not involve students in the assessment process. During formative assessment, students are intentionally involved as active self-assessors, goal-setters, and goal-getters. They need to be gathering information about their own learning process and progress. Formative assessment informs learning—it puts students in the driver's seat.

Reflecting on the Essential Elements of the Formative Assessment Process

Formative assessment is an intentional learning process that involves teachers and their students in an active partnership focused on improving achievement and generating motivation to learn. As you reflect on the kind of learning environment formative assessment will help teachers in your school create for and with their students, consider the following questions:

- Do both teachers and students intentionally focus on gathering evidence to inform student learning, or are teachers in charge of assessment efforts focused on auditing learning?
- Does everyone in the classroom share responsibility for learning, or is the teacher responsible for saying what has been learned, who has learned it, and what needs to be learned next?

- Are there classrooms where teachers and their students partner in the formative assessment process day to day and minute by minute? Are there classrooms where teachers are using one or two formative assessment strategies in stand-alone ways? Are there classrooms with little evidence of formative assessment? How can you encourage teachers to work together, share their thinking, and view each other as valuable resources as they individually and collectively work to improve the quality of the formative assessment process in their classrooms?

Summing It Up

The formative assessment process is lightning in a bottle! It costs nothing. You can help teachers put it to work for every age and grade level in every subject during each minute of every school day. This powerful learning process enhances the learning of those who are already excelling, jump-starts and sustains learners who are smoldering with potential, and increases student achievement for all students. What's more, formative assessment raises teacher quality and forges learning partnerships between students and teachers that make a huge difference in what happens every day and every minute in the classroom.

One word of encouragement and caution: Even lightning in a bottle takes time to impact the culture of a school. The formative assessment process, like any other reframing of what happens in classrooms, will take time to grow and develop. Keep in mind that it is a learning process for all learners in the school—the students, the teachers, and the administration. The good news is that when a school commits to creating learning opportunities like the ones we discuss in the remainder of the book, good things begin to happen immediately and multiply quickly. (Chapter 8 explores taking formative assessment schoolwide in greater detail.)

In the chapters that follow, we explore the six elements of the formative assessment process. Each chapter includes specific and practical strategies to help you give teachers both the research base and the how-to information that they will need to implement formative assessment in their own classrooms to increase student achievement and motivation to learn.

2

LEVELING THE PLAYING FIELD:
Sharing Learning Targets and Criteria for Success

The first step in formative assessment is being clear about learning goals. Actually, the first step in any kind of assessment is being clear about what it is that you want to know about. You may have heard this expressed as "identify outcomes" or in some other terminology used in your state or district. Simply put, if assessment is looking for evidence of something, you have to know what that something is.

For an external assessor, identifying outcomes is enough. For the classroom teacher, however, being clear about learning goals requires more than just identifying outcomes. For formative assessment, teachers not only must be clear about what they want students to learn (the lesson objective or intended outcome for students who "get it"); they also must know typical student steps and missteps toward this goal (the typical learning progression). This knowledge is necessary because what the teacher is looking for in formative assessment is evidence of where students are on their journey toward mastery of the learning outcome. To interpret student work that is on the way toward mastery, teachers need to be able to recognize typical and not-so-typical progress.

What Does It Mean to Share Learning Targets and Criteria for Success?

Sharing learning targets does not mean merely writing the objective on the board or telling students what the objective is in a sentence or two. Most students will, of course, be able to repeat back to the teacher what she said the objective was, and that can be somewhat useful. What we mean by sharing learning targets and criteria for success, however, is that students comprehend what those objectives mean. For example, a reading objective might be that students can identify the main idea in passages of a certain type and level. What we want is more than students being able to say "identify main idea." We want students to understand that they will learn how to get a better grasp on the meaning of what they read, why that should be a goal for them, and what it feels like to do that. For the student, this means both understanding the learning goal and knowing what good work on the assignment looks like. It's not a goal if the student can't envision it.

The single most important method for routinely sharing learning targets is using assignments that match—*really* match—the learning goal. It is in the assignment that the teacher translates the learning goal into action for the student. The student will strive to do the assignment, not the abstract goal. When we say an assignment or activity must "embody" the learning goal, we mean that the assignment or activity is such a close match with the goal that the student would be able to think, "If I can do [this assignment], then I can do [the learning objective]."

Teachers should always share their goals for students' learning—both by telling or writing the goals and by giving assignments and activities that embody them—and then check for students' understanding. It is not enough to ask students, "Do you understand?" They'll say yes, of course! Rather, teachers should use strategies that help assess students' comprehension of the meaning of learning goals and their comprehension of what good work looks like. Teachers should use this information to affirm understanding and clarify misconceptions.

How Does Sharing Learning Targets and Criteria for Success Affect Student Learning and Achievement?

One of the sweet moments in the life of one of the authors illustrates this question's point. Sue's adult daughter, newly on her own, asked Sue to make her a collection of the recipes that she had come to know and love (including Sue's apple pie and pot roast). Of course, it felt good to know that she associated these foods with home and wanted to take them with her to her own new home. But this homey story is a good metaphor for this chapter. Sue's daughter had a very clear picture of the intended outcome, based on her experiences of that pie and that pot roast over the years. She would compare her attempts to make these recipes with her sense of what they should taste like. Now, the pot roast was easy enough, but she had to practice several times to get the pie right. The point for this chapter is that if she did not have a concept of what "good" pie was, she would not have been able to shape her pie baking toward it, or at least not as effectively or efficiently.

Academic learning targets, although less concrete, work in a similar way. A vision of the end point makes the journey possible. So, for example, a 4th grade teacher might ask her students to write a book report. Her learning target, however, is not "write a book report." She wants students to be able to read and comprehend the plot of a chapter book and to be able to make a personal connection with the story. Therefore, she says, "Your book report should be two paragraphs. In the first paragraph, summarize the story so that someone who has not read the book would know what happened. In the second paragraph, tell what your favorite part of the story was, and why."

In so doing, this teacher has given clear directions. She has also made a start at sharing the learning target. All the students in her class may well understand what they are supposed to do. However, we can almost guarantee that there will be many different visions of what constitutes a good, clear summary of a book and an engaging description of one's favorite part.

What would help students envision the target more clearly? Showing students some good examples and having them discuss why they were good examples would help. Showing students examples of various quality levels and having them use comparison and contrast to order them and explain why some are better than others would be an even stronger strategy. Using rubrics with specific descriptions could help with either of these processes and would be a good default strategy if no examples were available.

Now the students are ready to start their book reports with a clear target in mind. They may use those rubrics and examples again, during their work, to self-assess. We will have more to say about student self-assessment in Chapter 5.

What Common Misconceptions Might Teachers Hold About Sharing Learning Targets and Criteria for Success?

Teachers are likely to hold at least two common misconceptions about sharing learning targets.

Misconception #1: Informing the students of the learning target by telling them what it is or by writing it on the board is sufficient. This is probably the most common misconception teachers might hold about sharing learning targets. Years ago, in a district where one of us taught, teachers were required to write their objectives on the board, and supervisors would observe to make sure the teachers did so. The assumption behind this practice is that writing the objective on the board puts the objective inside the students' heads. This is not a good assumption. Having students be able to recall or recite the objective is necessary but not sufficient for their understanding it.

Strategic talking points school leaders can use to address this misconception include the following:

- Most "lesson objectives" are written in language for teachers.
- Discussion about what a lesson objective means can help students express the objective in their own words and clarify the concept in their own minds.
- Students will understand best what a goal really means when they can see examples of good work.

Misconception #2: Sharing a rubric with students will ensure they understand the criteria for success. Sharing a rubric with students is a good start, but as with the objective, you need to check for student understanding of what the criteria mean. Some criteria are easy to understand—for example, "use at least three sources of information"—but things you can count are not always at the heart of a learning goal. Some criteria require the students to have more abstract, but arguably more important, concepts. Using the context of writing, for example, a rubric for "voice" might say, "Conveys a sense of the person behind the words." Reading that phrase does not mean students will necessarily recognize writing that conveys a sense of the person behind the words when they see it. Some students will need to be taught how to distinguish writing that does this well and less well.

School leaders who observe teachers writing the objective on the board without any discussion or follow-up with students might want to talk with those teachers to determine if they, in fact, believe this is a sufficient method for sharing learning targets. Similarly, school leaders who observe teachers passing out rubrics and moving on with the assumption that students can use them might likewise talk with those teachers.

Strategic talking points school leaders can use to address this misconception include the following:

- Rubrics are a good starting point because they organize the criteria for students into levels of description about various aspects of the work.
- You can find out how students comprehend what the descriptive levels of a rubric mean by asking them to state them in their own words.
- Students can learn to more precisely identify levels of quality when they see them by looking at examples of work.
- Students who can identify quality levels in sample papers are better at self-assessment and at producing desired levels of work themselves.

What Is the Motivation Connection?

Students who have clear pictures of the learning target and of the criteria for success are likely to also have a sense of what they can and should do to make their work measure up to those criteria and that goal. Clear learning targets direct both teachers *and students* toward specific goals. Students can meet goals only if they are actually working toward them, and they can't work toward them until they understand what they are.

Once students understand where they are headed, they are more likely to feel that they can be successful, can actually reach the goal. Students' belief that they can be successful at a particular task or assignment is called self-efficacy (Bandura, 1997). Students who have self-efficacy are more likely to persist in their work and especially more likely to persist in the face of challenge (Pajares, 1996).

When students feel that they understand the criteria by which their work will be judged, they also have some sense of control over their work and are poised to be strategic self-regulators. If I, the student author, understand that a good story needs a sense of voice that engages readers and makes them feel like I am a real person communicating with them, and if I (or someone else) read my story and find it flat and wooden, then I know I have work to do—and, more important, I know *what* work I have to do. That student decision ("My story lacks a vibrant voice, and I should revise it for that reason") is an example of self-regulation.

Notice that it takes both an understanding of the learning target (what "voice" is in writing) and an understanding of the criteria for success (recognizing writing with effective use of voice when we see it) to foster self-efficacy and self-regulation. If students understand the learning target but don't know what qualities will get them there, they are likely to feel discouraged.

What Are Specific Strategies I Can Share with Teachers?

Teachers can help students understand learning targets by the same means they use to help students understand anything: telling, showing, or discovering. "Telling" methods were popular for a while. The classic in this category is for teachers to write their lesson objectives on the board. This method is certainly better than not mentioning the learning target, which makes it a guessing game ("I wonder why we're doing this?"). But, as noted earlier, a problem with this method is that lesson objectives are often expressed in teacher language—for example, "The student will be able to do three-digit subtraction with borrowing." True sharing of learning targets involves getting students to comprehend what the learning target entails. As we have already said, many students, having read this objective on the board, could repeat it back but not tell you much about what it meant.

In this book, we concentrate on ways to share learning targets and criteria for success by showing this information to students or by having students discover this information for themselves. Directed student conversation can be a powerful way for students to develop comprehension of their learning target. Strategies that put information in written form enable teachers and students to review and refer to it. Both oral and written strategies are ways to get what's inside a student's head out into public space so that others can hear it or read it and respond. Figure 2.1 summarizes the strategies that we discuss in the following sections.

Questioning

Questioning, along with directed conversation, is one strategy for communicating learning targets. The strategy can be simple or elaborate, depending on the particular students and content. Sometimes all that is needed is that a teacher ask students what questions they have about an assignment.

FIGURE 2.1
Strategies for Sharing Learning Targets and Criteria for Success

General Strategy	Specific Tactics	Examples
Questioning	• Teachers check for understanding by asking for student questions or by asking students to put learning goals in their own words.	*Kevin, can you tell me one thing about the water cycle you already know? . . . Jacob, can you tell me one other thing about the water cycle? . . . Jaden, can you put those two things together so we have a definition of the water cycle?*
	• Teachers use directed discussion or warm-up questions.	*Why is it important to know about the water cycle?*
		What would a good report on the water cycle look like?
	• Students think-pair-share what they think they will be learning, why it's important, and how it relates to previous learning.	*Donna, what do you think of Matthew's idea about the way to do a picture of the water cycle?*
		How long would the report have to be to show you really understood the whole water cycle?
Planning and Envisioning	• Students list what they know and want to know.	*Groups working on water cycle reports plan a week of work, including library research, reading, writing, drawing, editing, and planning a presentation.*
	• Students make planning charts for individual or group work.	*Students use these planning charts to keep track of progress. The teacher uses these planning charts for interim assessment of student progress and for asking questions about what students learn along the way.*
		The teacher asks for interim assessments as checkpoints along the way—for example, a list of sources after library day, an outline as the report is planned, a draft as the report is written, a list of students' roles for an oral presentation.

FIGURE 2.1

Strategies for Sharing Learning Targets and Criteria for Success *(cont.)*

General Strategy	Specific Tactics	Examples
Using Examples	• Students look at good examples and make a list of what makes them good.	*Here are the five best water cycle reports from last year. What do you notice about them?* *Can you organize these things you notice into categories?*
	• Students look at a range of examples, sort them into quality levels, and write descriptions of the levels that turn into draft rubrics.	*Put these water cycle reports into three piles: Good, OK, and Not Good.* *What makes the Good ones good? How are the OK reports different from the Good ones? From the Not Good ones?*
Using Rubrics	• Students use teacher-made rubrics to assess examples.	*Here are some water cycle reports from last year. Discuss with your group how you would evaluate them using this rubric, and why.*
	• Students rephrase teacher-made rubrics into their own words.	*Here is the rubric we will use for your water cycle reports. How would you describe these qualities to another student?*
	• Students use rubrics to assess their own work and revise.	*How do you think your water cycle report measures up on this rubric? Use a highlighter to show the descriptions in the rubric that you think describe your work. Is there anything you want to revise?*

Listening to these questions can provide the teacher with some information about what the students think they are to do and what they are to learn.

A variation on simple questioning as a strategy to communicate the learning target is for the teacher to describe a lesson's target and an assignment or activity that embodies it and then to ask students to repeat what she said in their own words. Putting something in one's own words is a classic comprehension activity. In so doing, students will show how they are understanding what the teacher is asking them to do.

A slightly more complex version of this questioning strategy is to use a think-pair-share activity. The teacher can have pairs of students (1) explain what they think they are going to learn, in their own words, (2) explain why they think it is important, and (3) figure out at least one previous lesson topic this goal is related to. In whole-class discussion, the pairs share and discuss their answers and come to a class consensus for the three questions (*What are you going to learn? Why is it important? What previous lesson topic is this goal related to?*). The purpose of the third question is to explicitly help students see that they are building knowledge and skill and to activate relevant prior knowledge that they can then use as they work.

Sato and Atkin (2006/2007) report on a version of this activity that they call "warm-up questions." The teacher prepares warm-up questions that review the previous lesson or preview the coming lesson. As students respond, the teacher asks students to comment on their peers' ideas and clarify or extend them. This directed discussion brings students' ideas about the learning target out into the open, where they can be examined and focused until everyone is clear on what the upcoming lesson is going to be about. An important feature of this strategy is that the teacher should discuss with students what high-quality responses to these questions would sound like. Students will not immediately be good "clarifiers and extenders." This skill needs to be developed.

When teachers use questioning as a strategy for clarifying a learning target, they should ask students about their attitudes and experiences as well as their knowledge. Teachers can ask students to describe what prior school or other experiences and what attitudes and feelings come to mind, as appropriate to the topic. They can assess students' responses for relevance and then use the information for adjusting instruction. For example, many elementary school students study recycling as a community activity or as part of a science unit. It would be useful to know which students come from homes where recycling is an important activity, what they do at home to recycle, and why their parents have told them they are doing it.

Planning and Envisioning

For some learning targets, having students envision what they know and what they will know (or do) can be a good way to give them a picture of what their learning will be about. The *K* and *W* columns ("know" and "want to know") of a KWL chart are classic examples of this strategy for clarifying learning targets.

For younger students, teachers can use actual pictures that are images for "what we will do" or "what we will need" (for example, a crystal ball might represent what they think an assignment will be about, and a tool box might represent the supplies they think they will need). Dictated or student-written words can be added to the pictures in appropriate places. Colored pictures can be used as cover sheets for folders of work, as appropriate.

For older students doing project work, planning charts for individual or group work can help clarify the learning target. Students must identify what needs to be done before they can plan how to do it. Such planning charts help more with the logistical aspects of the work than with understanding concepts, but they can be important steps along the way.

Using Examples

Giving students examples of work to review and describe helps them discover and develop conceptions of the learning target and criteria for good work by induction. If possible, teachers can use real examples from previous years from anonymous students. If no real examples from previous students are available, teachers can construct examples to illustrate the range of possible performance. If a teacher is using a rubric, it should include at least one example per level; two is better at the common levels of performance. For learning targets involving higher-order thinking, the teacher should try to have these represent levels of quality rather than quantity, so students will have to explain characteristics of the work rather than just say things like "You wanted three sources, and this paper only has two."

For some learning targets, a good source of anonymous examples that range in quality from excellent to poor is the National Assessment of Educational Progress released items, available at http://nces.ed.gov/nationsreportcard/itmrls/. Use the Questions Tool to bring up released items and examples of student work. Be sure to select "constructed response" (that is, not multiple-choice items) so there will be student work associated with the writing prompts, math problems, or social studies and science questions.

Students can discuss the qualities of the examples and arrive at a description of what good work looks like. If the teacher gave students a rubric, students can come to consensus on where each example would fall on the rubric, and why.

If the teacher has not given students a rubric, students can sort the examples into piles, come up with a description of each pile, and thus develop their own draft rubrics. For example, students can sort examples of work into "Good," "OK," and "Not Good" piles and then describe the characteristics of each. Teachers can use the student-generated rubrics as is or edit them as necessary. Even 1st graders can create rubrics in this way. Research suggests young children's first attempts at rubrics might give neatness and appearance too much weight and substance too little weight (Higgins, Harris, & Kuehn, 1994), but even this can make a teachable moment.

One of us met a teacher in Nebraska who had used the strategy of providing examples and "created a monster," as she said with a smile. Each year, her middle school science students created a notebook about the material they were studying. She decided to save some of the good science notebooks to use as examples, with student permission, of course. She found her students were eager to have her use their work as good examples. However, by her third year of using this strategy, she found that each year the notebooks were better than the year before. Students would look at the examples, figure out what the previous students had done, and go one better. The notebooks developed to be not only longer but also more substantive, because using examples made it easy for students to envision what could be done.

Sharing only good examples helps students envision a target. Sharing a range of examples, from good to poor, allows students to develop a conceptual understanding of the criteria. In the Nebraska example, if the teacher had shown students some mediocre and poor notebooks, too, the students would have had more opportunity to discuss the criteria. However, identifying a student's work as "not a good example" is something some teachers are reluctant to do, for the sake of the student. For a range of examples, it is best to use examples from anonymous sources or teacher-created examples.

Using Rubrics

The strategy of using examples often involves rubrics—either ones the teacher has provided or ones the students generate from the examples. Even if examples are not available, however, rubrics can help clarify learning targets in students' minds and help them understand the criteria for success. In some cases, student translations of teacher rubrics into what is sometimes called "kid-friendly" language can be helpful as well.

Teachers can also use rubrics to clarify learning targets through opportunities for revision, if appropriate. Students can review their own work against rubrics, decide what needs to be revised for improvement, and then do that before they turn in the work. Alternatively, the teacher can allow "not acceptable" papers or projects to be redone, although it is usually better for students to revise work before they turn it in for a grade. That makes them, and not the teacher, the arbiters of their revisions. Some teachers have students do peer review and revision. We advise that even if teachers incorporate peer review into their students' work time, they also allow for self-assessment. Peers can make helpful suggestions, but it is the students' own decisions about their work that lead to learning.

How Will I Recognize Effective Sharing of Learning Targets and Criteria for Success When I See It?

First, ask students. Probably the most accurate marker of classrooms where learning targets and criteria are shared effectively is that students can explain, when asked, what it is that they are supposed to do, and why.

Second, observe teachers. Look for evidence that the strategies described in the preceding sections—questioning, planning and envisioning, using examples, and using rubrics—are being not only used but used well. In particular, look for the following:

- Are students asked to put the learning targets (or lesson objectives) in their own words?
- Are students asked to talk about their ideas and previous experiences related to learning targets?
- Does the teacher listen to student visions of their work, and, more important, does the teacher use that information in some way?
- Are students encouraged to plan their work, and do they have opportunities to implement those plans?
- Do students have an opportunity to review and respond to examples of work?
- Does the teacher use rubrics formatively—that is, to shape work, not just to grade it?

Learning to recognize the ways that teachers and students share learning targets requires systematic observation based on a clear understanding of the many effective ways this sharing can happen. Such observation can also help you uncover areas for professional growth that can guide your conversations with teachers about the critical importance of sharing learning targets and the criteria for success. The exercise presented here—a shared learning targets case study—is a three-tiered process for gathering sound evidence through a classroom walk-through (see Figure 2.2), a lesson plan/assignment walk-through (see Figure 2.3), and a student outcome walk-through (see Figure 2.4), followed by documentation of conclusions and determination of goals and strategies (see Figure 2.5). The exercise will help you document the ways teachers are clearly communicating the learning target and criteria for success and how students are using that information to learn how to learn—to become confident and competent self-regulated learners. Although the case study format is designed to assist a classroom walk-through, you can also use it to guide a more comprehensive formal classroom observation.

How Can I Model Effective Sharing of Learning Targets and Criteria for Success in Conversations with Teachers About Their Own Professional Learning?

Teachers should have the same clarity about your goals for them as you expect them to have about their goals for students. Often teachers are given professional

FIGURE 2.2

Tier 1: Classroom Walk-Through for Sharing Learning Targets

Document the ways the teacher communicates learning targets and the criteria for success/elements of quality with students. You can use notes to expand on your observations.			
The teacher used the following communication modes to share the learning targets and criteria for success/elements of quality:			
❏ Oral	❏ Written	❏ Displays	❏ Demonstrations/ modeling
The teacher used the following formats to share the learning targets and the criteria for success:			
❏ Rubric	❏ Contract	❏ Checklist of expectations and requirements	❏ Anchor papers, models, or other exemplars of quality

When did the teacher communicate the learning targets and the criteria for success?		
❏ Before instruction	❏ During instruction/ongoing	❏ At the conclusion of instruction

How did the teacher help the students to understand the learning targets and the criteria for success/elements of quality?		
❏ Conducted discussion and review	❏ Discussed criteria, rubrics, checklists	❏ Showed student work, modeled responses, examined exemplars or anchors of quality
❏ Helped students apply the criteria to their own work or to a model	❏ Involved students in generating criteria/elements of quality	❏ Provided feedback to students that focused on the learning target and the criteria for success

In what ways did the teacher engage the students in applying the criteria for success/elements of quality?			
❏ Helped students compare their work to anchors or exemplars	❏ Helped students identify anchors or models based on the criteria	❏ Used rubrics, checklists, or other tools to assist in assessments of quality	❏ Helped students develop criteria for success/elements of quality

In what ways did the teacher engage the students in developing/identifying criteria for success and/or elements of quality?		
❏ Brainstormed/discussed criteria	❏ Discussed elements of quality directly related to the learning target and performance task/product requirements	❏ Discussed elements of a quality answer, paper, response, *A* work

FIGURE 2.3

Tier 2: Classroom Walk-Through for Lesson Plans and Learning Activities on Sharing Learning Targets

Use the continuums to plot the evidence from the design elements of the lesson plan(s) showing the teacher takes a systematic and intentional approach to communicating learning targets and criteria for success/elements of quality with students.

Clearly Defined Learning Targets

The plan's learning targets represent activities rather than learning outcomes and cannot be assessed.

The plan's learning targets define observable and measurable outcomes and can be assessed.

○   ○   ○   ○   ○   ○   ○

Alignment of Assessment Plans

The plan's assessment strategies are not aligned with the learning targets. Or the plan does not contain assessment strategies that will provide evidence of the effects on student learning.

The plan's assessment strategies are aligned with the learning targets and will provide strong evidence of the effects on student learning.

○   ○   ○   ○   ○   ○   ○

Learning Activities

The planned learning experiences are not related to the learning targets.

The planned learning experiences are strongly tied to the learning targets and help students build capacity to close the gap between where they are and where they need to go.

○   ○   ○   ○   ○   ○   ○

Feedback That Feeds Forward

The plan provides no opportunities for students to receive feedback that feeds them forward as they learn how to regulate their performance to reach the criteria for success/elements of quality.

The plan provides for feedback during the learning experiences that helps students regulate their performance to meet the criteria for success/elements of quality.

○   ○   ○   ○   ○   ○   ○

Student Engagement

The plan provides no opportunities for students to examine the learning targets and the criteria for success/elements of quality by reviewing and responding to examples of work.

The plan provides opportunities for students to actively examine the learning targets and the criteria for success/elements of quality by reviewing and responding to examples of work in order to plan their work and implement their plans.

○   ○   ○   ○   ○   ○   ○

FIGURE 2.4
Tier 3: Classroom Walk-Through for Student Outcomes on Sharing Learning Targets

Document the student outcomes that provide strong evidence that the teacher communicates the learning targets and the criteria for success/elements of quality with students.

Ask three students the following question: *What are you learning in this lesson?* **Then check all that apply:**

❏ Students describe what they are doing rather than what they are learning.
   Examples: *We are writing papers. We are working problems. We are finishing our projects.*
❏ Students describe what they are learning in general terms.
   Examples: *We are learning about weather. We are learning math. We are learning about dogs.*
❏ Students provide a clear and accurate description of what they are learning.
   Examples: *We are learning to write a topic sentence. We are learning the functions of the circulatory system.*

Ask three students the following questions: *Are you doing well (or doing a good job) on this task? How do you know?* **Then check all that apply:**

❏ Students cannot describe the criteria for success/elements of quality.
   Examples: *I don't know. I will know when I see my grade. I will ask the teacher for help.*
❏ Students describe a general strategy for assessing the quality of their work.
   Examples: *I will do a good job if I follow directions; answer all the questions; do my best.*
❏ Students describe specific strategies for assessing the quality of their work.
   Examples: *I use the steps in the chart. I refer to the rubric. I look at the examples of good work. I use the checklist. I try to make mine like the model the teacher gave us.*

Examine student products connected to the lesson. Then check all that apply:

❏ The lesson will not result in student products that can be assessed for learning progress toward the learning target.
❏ The students will produce work that has minimal to no connection to the learning targets.
❏ The students will produce work that provides strong evidence of their progress toward the learning target.
❏ Students will have the opportunity to incorporate feedback or use tools (rubrics, checklists, etc.) to refine and revise their work in order to meet the criteria for success/elements of quality connected to the learning target.

Examine the homework assignment connected to the lesson. Then check all that apply:

❏ Homework assignments are strongly connected to the learning targets.
❏ Homework assignments are paired with a way for students to judge the quality of their work.
❏ Homework assignments will help students close the gap between where they are in relation to the learning target.

Ask the teacher the following question: *In this lesson, how do you share the learning targets and criteria for success/elements of quality with your students?* **Record the response.**

FIGURE 2.5
Conclusions and Goal Setting for Learning Targets Case Study

1. Based on the evidence you gathered through the three-tiered Learning Targets Walk-Through, what are your conclusions regarding the quality, consistency, and effect of the ways the teacher shares the learning targets and success criteria in order to inform student learning and increase student achievement?

2. Based on your conclusions above, what are three specific goals that you have for this teacher?

Goal 1:

Goal 2:

Goal 3:

3. Given the professional goals above, state three specific strategies you can share to help the teacher become more effective at sharing learning targets and the criteria for success.

Strategy 1:

Strategy 2:

Strategy 3:

development expectations without a clear idea of what it is they should "develop." We also know that professional learning goals for teachers can be more or less thoughtful. One of us once did some work in a high school that required teachers to submit professional development goals and plans at the beginning of the year. One teacher wrote "be more professional" as his goal, and as evidence, he was going to count the number of days he wore a tie to school. Sadly, this really happened.

The first tip for learning targets for teacher professional development is to base them on individual teachers' needs—or better, to arrive at mutually agreed-upon professional development goals based on your observations, the teacher's reflections, and joint conversation about the goals. If a goal is partly the result of teacher self-assessment, all those motivational benefits about feelings of control and being the agent of one's own destiny will kick in.

Communicate with the teacher not only what you think the professional development goal should be but also what evidence makes that an important goal. One of the questioning strategies we described earlier is a good one to use. Simply asking the teacher to describe what it is she wants to improve, in her own words, and what she plans to do about it will go a long way in most cases to making sure that the teacher understands the goal and that the teacher knows you know she understands the goal.

Following right along, let the teacher know what you will interpret as evidence that the goal has been met and what criteria you will use. It would be even better if the evidence and criteria could be arrived at jointly, in conversation. Remember that conversation is a means by which the thinking in one person's head can be brought to light so that others can reflect and comment. Conversation in this sense is a real give and take, not a grilling or a lecture. Conversation is also the means by which people indicate their understanding of whatever they are talking about. So talking about evidence and criteria with the teacher may actually serve as a means to clarify ideas for both you and the teacher.

What If?

Communicating learning targets involves teachers and students. Teachers must have a clear conception of the target, send clear messages about it, and provide clear opportunities for students to develop the concept. Like teachers, students have to be able to understand and work with the concept behind the learning target. *What if you ask a student to explain the learning target he is working toward and the student can't come up with an answer?*

First, gather additional evidence. Is it one student who cannot express a clear concept of the learning target, or are many students in the same boat? Does the teacher know that this student doesn't understand, or does she assume he does? In short, try to determine if the issue is that the teacher needs to take a differentiated approach with one or a few students, or if the lack of understanding represents something more wide-ranging. If it's one or a few students, talk with the teacher about strategies for individualizing learning.

If many students cannot say what the learning target is, gather some additional evidence and do some triangulation. Look at three different sources. What do the teacher's lesson plans say the learning target is? When asked, what does the teacher say it is? What do the lesson activities and assignments imply that it is? If these three do not agree, there's the problem: there is no clear learning target. Start there with the teacher, focusing on how to develop good learning targets (Gronlund & Brookhart, 2009). Talk with the teacher about the importance of coherence in planning, instruction, and assessment. Sometimes that is all it takes. For example, a teacher may have grabbed a worksheet that looked like a match— maybe it was about the same topic, for example, butterflies—without analyzing the work required to make sure it dealt with the same specific concepts or required the same thinking skills. Sometimes teachers need practice at analyzing what really is required of students in an activity or assignment, and you can work on that.

And finally, sometimes the three sources of information do agree, but they describe activities, not learning targets. For example, the teacher may say, "We're doing posters about Canada," without having a clear sense beyond that. Of course, then the students would probably have said, "We're making posters," instead of being able to state the learning goal. Is the goal to learn facts about Canada? To understand the relationship between the United States and Canada? To understand interdependencies among two countries in North America? Something else? In that case, explore with the teacher how activities and assignments should be instances that embody the learning target, selected from a group of possible activities and assignments in service of the same knowledge or skill. In our experience, you will run into this issue a lot. Many teachers use activities as a shorthand for learning goals, which unfortunately will have the effect of limiting learning.

Reflecting on Sharing Learning Targets and Criteria for Success

There is no more foundational activity for a school leader than making sure that there are clear learning targets aligned to whatever standards are in place in the school or district, that teachers understand them and teach to them, and that students understand them and reach for them. Reflect on these questions for your school or district:

- Are there classrooms where students understand their goals particularly well? Conversely, are there classrooms where activities just seem to happen to get "done"? What are the differences in how students work and how they behave in those two types of classrooms?
- Do some teachers struggle with the concept of a "learning goal"? With the idea of an activity or assignment tapping into that learning goal in a deep way? For those teachers, what is the level of their own content knowledge and of their knowledge of typical student learning progressions for that topic?
- Do you observe a range of student behavior in the classrooms in your school? Is there any relationship between the number and type of behavior problems in a class and the clarity of student understanding and teacher communication of learning goals?

Summing It Up

In this chapter, we have talked about the foundation of formative (and summative, too, for that matter) assessment—clear communication of learning targets and clear understanding of the criteria for success. In fact, it is this characteristic— that they are both based on the same learning goals—that relates formative and summative assessment in education. We have discussed strategies teachers might use to share learning targets and criteria with their students. After that point in most lesson sequences, the students get busy and do some work. In Chapter 3, then, we turn to ways to give feedback to students on that work so that their learning can continue to progress.

3

SHIFTING FROM CORRECTING TO INFORMING:
Feedback That Feeds Forward

Educators have been studying feedback for almost 100 years. The first studies and theories about feedback grew out of the psychological perspective called behaviorism. Positive feedback was "reinforcement," and negative feedback was "punishment." As the heyday of behaviorism waned, researchers tried to understand more about why feedback worked. Several reviewers found little support for the behaviorist notion that feedback was simple reinforcement but definite support for the idea that correcting errors was an important way in which feedback worked (Bangert-Drowns, Kulik, Kulik, & Morgan, 1991; Kluger & DeNisi, 1996; Kulhavy, 1977).

We now know that error correction is an important feedback function but not the only one. More recently, studies and theories about feedback have found a place in cognitive psychology, especially in the notion that feedback helps students with self-regulation of learning (Butler & Winne, 1995) by helping them understand the learning goal, how close their current work comes to it, and what should be done next (Hattie & Timperley, 2007). Of course, you recognize these as the three components of the formative assessment cycle.

What Is Feedback?

Feedback, in the sense we are using it here, is a teacher's response to student work with the intention of furthering learning. Feedback can be written or oral, or it can be a demonstration. Teachers can give feedback about many different things, but in this book we focus on teacher feedback to students on their academic work: classroom activities and assignments, written work, homework, tests, projects, and so on. We focus on feedback to students about this work that can be part of the formative assessment cycle—that is, it is based on the criteria from specific learning goals, descriptive of where the student's work falls in this regard, and suggestive of ways to improve or learn more.

In the language of the self-regulation theorists, feedback is "external regulation"—external to the learner. Feedback from a teacher becomes part of the information students use for "internal regulation" and learning. Thus no matter how good a teacher's feedback is, it doesn't guarantee that students learn. However, feedback creates opportunities for students to grow by giving them insights about their work that they might not be able to come up with on their own.

Effective feedback is a teacher's response to student work using the criteria for good work that were part of the learning target. Effective feedback observes where the work did a good job of meeting the criteria and where it did not. Effective feedback suggests ways the student could go about understanding the reasons for these observations, building on strengths and improving weaknesses.

How Does Feedback Affect Student Learning and Achievement?

Effective feedback affects student learning in two ways. First, information from clear, descriptive feedback supports achievement. As the students better understand where they are in relation to the learning target and take the next steps, their work improves. Feedback supports cognition because it helps students realize which knowledge and skills are strong and which are weak. More subtly, feedback can help move students from misconceptions to clearer understanding through targeted explanation of particular points and suggestions about what (or how) to study or practice next. Feedback also supports metacognition—students' awareness about their own thinking and their use of this self-awareness to regulate their thinking. Feedback shows students their work from an outsider's point of view. Effective feedback shows students how to look at their work using criteria from the assignment and thus, by modeling, helps teach them self-assessment skills.

Second, information from clear, descriptive feedback supports motivation. Students who see that improvement is something they can control—because they understand what to do next—are motivated to take those steps. Feelings of competence and autonomy are powerful motivators to productive action for all of us (Ryan & Deci, 2000), and especially for students. We say "especially for students" because many school assignments put students in the position of being told what to do. Effective feedback that helps *them* decide what to do can feel particularly liberating.

What Common Misconceptions Might Teachers Hold About Feedback?

Teachers typically hold at least two common misconceptions about feedback.

Misconception #1: Returning graded work is providing effective feedback. Some teachers view feedback as grading or marking (as expressed in the comment "I marked and returned their papers"). It is true that knowledge of results, sometimes called "outcome feedback," is a basic kind of feedback. With this kind of feedback, however, many students are more interested in how many questions they "got right" than in understanding the reasons behind their performance. Successful students may try to figure out why certain answers were wrong or why they got a certain grade—but successful students usually get good grades and few wrong answers. The effective feedback we discuss in this book is not grading.

Strategic talking points school leaders can use to address this misconception include the following:

- Some students will look seriously at the feedback on graded work, but many will just look at the grade.
- In the typical classroom sequence of learning activities, by the time a graded assignment is due to be turned in, the optimum time for feedback has passed. It is too late.
- Students experience grading as evaluation and judgment. To be most effective, feedback must be experienced as information and description.

Misconception #2: Detailed correction is effective feedback. Did you ever have an English teacher whose feedback on your essay looked like copyediting?

All the spelling, punctuation, and usage errors were corrected, and all you had to do to have a "perfect" paper was recopy the essay using your teacher's corrections. In math, problems that are corrected without explanation—so the student knows what the answers are but not why—have the same effect on students. In any subject, feedback that supplies the "right" answer for students instead of inviting them into some learning process that will help them understand the work is not effective.

Strategic talking points school leaders can use to address this misconception include the following:

- When a teacher "fixes" all mistakes or copyedits written work, the student does not get an opportunity to figure anything out.
- Students can revise work according to teacher corrections without actually understanding why the corrected versions are better.
- Effective feedback describes types of strengths and deficiencies in work and suggests strategies the student might use to take next steps.

What Is the Motivation Connection?

As described in the overview in Chapter 1, effective feedback enhances students' cognitive processing, increases students' autonomy, fosters resiliency and persistence, and provides students with specific strategies for next steps in their learning. Here is a simple example. Instead of inserting a period on a student's paper, a teacher might ask, "Where does this sentence end?" This question tells the student what needs to be figured out next and implies the student can do it. That may be all the student needs. Or if not, a next question could be "What punctuation mark goes at the end of that sentence?" The principles for good feedback are easy to see in a simple example, and they generalize to more complex work.

Feedback enhances cognitive processing by providing needed information. For example, feedback may inform a successful 5th grade student that his teacher knows he included many details in his paragraph comparing and contrasting two characters in a story. Feedback may inform an unsuccessful 5th grade student that she did not report facts from the story accurately. Knowing these things will help both students in their next comparison/contrast assignment.

Feedback provides students with specific strategies for next steps in their learning. Once students understand the next steps, they are more likely to take them. Knowledge is power, as the saying goes. For example, the teacher may suggest that the unsuccessful student reread the story and use underlining as a strategy for identifying details and reporting them accurately. If the student knows how to underline, she might think, "Oh, I could do that."

Feedback increases students' autonomy and persistence in their work by giving them the evidence they need to believe that they are, in fact, competent—and where they are not yet competent, giving them the means to become so. The successful 5th grader in our example, after reading his teacher's comments, knows that his use of detail is serving him well. This will make him more likely to repeat that kind of performance in the future. Even the unsuccessful student, who may take a while to develop into a successful reader and writer, will have more direction next time because she is now armed with some suggestions (check facts, reread, underline details) that give her somewhere to start. The next assignment may seem like an easier task for this student, one that she may feel will work out better for her, than it would have been if the teacher had simply disapproved of the work and not provided that feedback.

What Are Specific Strategies I Can Share with Teachers?

Teachers have various choices about the methods they use when they deliver feedback and about the content of that feedback.

Methods of Feedback

The choices about methods relate to the following areas:

- Timing—when given; how often
- Amount—how many points are made; how much about each point
- Mode—oral; written; visual/demonstration
- Audience—individual; group/class

Timing. Students should get feedback while they are still mindful of the learning target and while there is still time for them to act on it. Feedback should be given as soon as possible for right/wrong questions and as soon as feasible for more complex products like papers or projects. Feedback can also be given after cumulative observations. For example, if many or most of the math problems a student turns in contain careless errors, it would be worthwhile for the teacher to say something such as this: "George, I see you read right over this question. I have noticed you doing that on previous papers, too. What can you do to slow down your reading and make sure you do your work completely?"

Amount. The right amount of feedback to give is different for different students and assignments. The idea is for students to get enough feedback that they have a sense of the teacher's response to the work against the assignment's criteria and enough feedback so that they know what to do next. The right amount of feedback for one student might overwhelm another. A teacher should select a couple of main points for comment and then take stock. Is that enough? Is there more that should be said to this student? For example, if a teacher has been working all week with a student on careful work habits and the student turns in a carefully done paper, the teacher should tell her she noticed.

Comments should be made on at least as many strengths as weaknesses. Teachers should make sure to comment on "teachable moment" points, too. Even for unsuccessful students, the teacher should name and notice at least one good thing the student did.

Mode. The most appropriate feedback may be written or oral, or even a demonstration. It depends on the learning target, the assignment, and the age and verbal abilities of the student. Oral feedback works best for very young students or for students who are not apt to read what is written, or if the teacher has so much to say that the effect of seeing it in writing would be overwhelming.

On the other hand, written feedback is more permanent than oral feedback. Students can keep it and refer to it as they do their work. Written feedback works well for students who can use it as they revise essays, papers, or projects. Written feedback can be inserted at specific points in written work, in margins, using arrows or underlining, and so on, so the student knows where the comments apply. For these reasons, it makes sense for teachers to use written feedback as often as possible and *also* to use oral feedback. Even students who read well will respond to good feedback delivered orally as a teacher walks around while students work in class, for example.

For some things, demonstration is the best mode. Physical skills, of course, cry out for demonstration—for example, for young children learning to hold a pencil or tie shoes or music students learning how to hold an instrument. Demonstration in the form of modeling is a good way to "show" a student how to exercise cognitive skills. For example, if a student's writing would benefit from more vivid vocabulary, a teacher could say, "Use more vivid details." Or she could demonstrate: "Instead of just saying the boy fell off his bicycle, it might sound more interesting if you added details. How about, 'The boy clutched the handlebars helplessly as he lost his balance and fell from his bicycle to the hard street below'?"

Audience. Feedback can be delivered to one, some, or many students. Specific, personal critiques should be delivered to individual students. Individual feedback has the additional value of communicating that the teacher read and responded to the student's work. If feedback feels "just for me," it can communicate that the teacher values that student's learning and cares about her progress, as well as communicating the content of the feedback words. Individual feedback should start with comments about what the student did well and then give comments about what needs improvement.

Whole-group feedback that is really aimed at only a few students is usually ineffective. It turns off the students who know they don't need it, confuses the students who aren't sure whether they need it or not, and may be ignored by the students the teacher intends to reach. But there are times when all members of a group need to hear the same thing. This often amounts to a minilesson that reteaches some concept to a small group of students pulled together because they have a common learning need, as in a flex group.

Content of Feedback

Teachers also have choices about the content of the feedback they give. These choices relate to the following areas:

- Focus—the work itself; the process the student used; the student personally
- Function—description; evaluation/judgment

- Comparison—with criteria for good work, *criterion-referenced*; with the work of other students, *norm-referenced*; with the student's own past performance, *self-referenced*
- Valence—positive; negative
- Clarity—clear to the student; unclear to the student
- Specificity—nitpicky; just right; overly general
- Tone—implications; what the student will "hear"

Focus. Feedback needs to be a message *about* something. What should a teacher focus on? First, the teacher should describe the work the student did in terms of the criteria the student was expected to meet. If the criteria were captured in a rubric that the teacher shared with students, the teacher should use the rubric's categories for feedback. For example, "Nice job" isn't very descriptive, and it isn't focused on particular criteria. On the other hand, "This project is nicely organized according to Galileo's scientific contributions" describes the project according to one of its criteria (organization), tells the student the teacher believes the criterion was well met, and tells the student why (it was clear that the structure of the project was built around Galileo's scientific contributions, as opposed to chronologically or other ways the project could have been organized). It is all right to comment "Good work!" if the comment goes on to say why the work was good.

If possible, teachers should talk about both the quality of the work and the process they observed (or can infer) that the student used to do the work. In some subjects, processes are more visible and more a part of lessons than others, but all subjects involve processes. For example, reading teachers typically teach reading strategies (sounding out words, using context clues, and so on). Mathematics teachers typically teach algorithms and methods for different types of problems. In these cases, commenting on the process is fairly obvious.

Work in all subjects requires a process of some sort, however. To return to our Galileo project example, suppose the feedback had gone on to say that some of Galileo's achievements were more clearly described than others. In addition to describing what specific achievements the teacher was referring to, her feedback could include some comments about the process of finding information. Especially helpful would be feedback suggesting additional information-finding procedures that the student could have used, or suggestions that help develop self-regulation, like taking stock to see whether additional information was needed at various points during the work.

Function. Feedback can be descriptive or evaluative, thereby making students feel enlightened or judged. A teacher should aim for descriptive feedback that students will perceive as information to help them with their work and avoid evaluative feedback that students will perceive as judgmental or bossy.

This can be easier said than done. A teacher's choice of comments is a big part of whether feedback is descriptive or not. For example, "There is only one event in this story" seems descriptive. "Not good enough!" seems judgmental. But in the end, it is the student's perception of the feedback that makes it descriptive or evaluative. Fragile students sometimes hear descriptive feedback as a judgment ("I'm stupid") even when that was not what the teacher said. For those students, it is especially important for the teacher to communicate every achievement, however small, so they begin to see themselves as people who *can* do something.

Comparison. Descriptions of work need some sort of basis or comparison. Feedback can compare work with criteria (called *criterion-referenced* feedback), with the work of other students (*norm-referenced* feedback), or with the student's own past performance or expectations for current performance (*self-referenced* feedback).

Criterion-referenced feedback, using as criteria the qualities of good work that were part of the learning target, is usually best for learning. For example, "The contour lines on your topographical map are not all in the right places" is criterion-referenced feedback. "Your topographical map is not as good as most of the other kids' maps" is norm-referenced feedback.

Self-referenced feedback can help all students as they progress toward developmental (long-term) learning targets such as developing writing or research skills. Pointing out what students did well and how this compares with the last time the teacher observed them use the same skill can help students set goals, build on strengths, and work on weaknesses.

For fragile students, self-referenced feedback can be a way to point out progress even when the work itself is not very good. For example, suppose a student wrote a very poor report on the stars, but at least she used one source and had some accurate information. Suppose further that her previous report on the planets had been mostly made up from things she had heard in class. Instead of a teacher describing how the poor report on stars didn't meet the criteria she had set, her feedback could focus on the aspects of this report that she noted as improvements over the last one. A teacher's noticing and naming accomplishments can be valuable as affirmations for students who do not believe they can do much in school. The criteria come into play—the comments are about aspects of the work such as use of sources and accuracy of information—but the focus is on the student's improvement. This kind of feedback helps students see the connection between their effort and their achievement. It gives the teacher the opportunity to affirm any progress, however small, and suggest next steps.

Norm-referenced feedback is almost never helpful for learning. Comparing students with one another sets up a competitive classroom atmosphere where "getting it right" and outdoing one's classmates are more important than understanding concepts or developing skills. Comparing students with one another encourages students to hide misunderstandings so they won't be found wanting, and in so doing they also miss opportunities to clear up those misunderstandings in class. Comparing students with one another also encourages students to believe that intelligence is innate rather than learned, and students who don't believe they can learn won't learn much.

Valence. Feedback comments should be positive, not negative. Positive comments include affirmations noticing and naming good qualities in a student's work. Positive comments also include descriptions of places where the work needs improvement coupled with suggestions for how to do that, sometimes called "constructive criticism." Negative comments, simply describing the bad qualities of a student's work without offering any assistance, are not effective. If the student had known how to do better, he probably would have.

We should add one caution. A teacher should not give in to the temptation to tell a student that work is good simply because she doesn't have the heart to tell him it's not. That may be easier in the short term, but it's a disaster in the long run. The teacher should just make sure she doesn't criticize any aspect of poor work without giving specific, forward-looking help in the very next breath.

Clarity. Feedback needs to be clear *to the student*. This may sound obvious, but it's important to consider what the student will understand. If the student didn't understand something the way the teacher explained it in class, simply repeating those words on the student's paper will not lead to improvement. If the teacher is not sure whether a student understands some feedback, she should check—and not by simply saying "Do you understand?" (because the student will say yes). She should really check. For example, the teacher could ask the student to tell in his own words what he will do next.

Specificity. Feedback should be specific enough to be helpful, but not so specific that the work is done for the student. Remember our example of written papers where the teacher copyedits everything? Not good. Sometimes using examples is an effective way to make feedback specific for a student.

Tone. The way a teacher addresses a student communicates a lot. Brusque, order-giving comments ("Do this! Do that!") convey that the teacher thinks a student should be ordered around. Sometimes well-meaning teachers who are pressed for time write feedback that sounds like orders even when that's not what they intended.

The teacher should aim for feedback that personalizes the students and positions them as the agent of their own learning. Feedback should imply that the person being addressed is a decision-making, autonomous being who is actively involved in figuring out how to learn. This really is a case of "you get what you wish for." When teachers treat students as if they are agents of their own learning, in most cases they will respond in kind. For example, if a student did a skimpy report on the electoral college, a teacher could say, "This needs to be longer." That certainly communicates what needs to be done. But it also communicates "Your report needs to be longer because I said so." If instead the teacher said, "After I read this, I wanted to know more. What could you add?" she sends the message that the report needs to be longer. But she also sends the message that it is the student's decisions that will make that happen and asks the student a question that will begin that process.

The Metaphor of Nutritional Value

Borrowing the concept of nutritional value provides an apt and vivid metaphor to focus teacher attention on the characteristics of high-quality feedback. For feedback to feed forward, it must have nutritional value. Food that is fresh and full of nutrients, prepared in a way that is healthy and inviting, served in a proportion that is appropriate, and provided as part of a balanced diet has a great deal of nutritional value. Effective feedback shares these characteristics. As we have already discussed, it must, among other things, be timely, appropriate, descriptive, and an integral part of the formative assessment process.

Ask teachers to think about the nutritional value in one serving of their feedback. Does it meet student learning needs in ways that feed the student forward? Using a checklist or chart like the one in Figure 3.1 can help teachers not only see how feedback strategies work together but also understand what we mean when we talk about using high-quality feedback to effectively feed the learning forward.

How Will I Recognize Effective Feedback When I See It?

We have just discussed the qualities of effective feedback. One way to recognize it, then, is to look for those qualities in teacher feedback. Look for feedback that is

- Timely.
- Not too much or too little, making at least one observation about a strength of the work.

FIGURE 3.1
What Is the Nutritional Value of One Serving of Your Feedback?

Feedback Nutrition Facts

Serving Size: Feedback on one performance

Amount: Just right	
Rate how well the feedback...	
	% of Nutritional Value
Compared the student's work with the learning target:	
Described what the student did well:	
Suggested a specific strategy for next steps:	
Arrived as soon as possible after the performance:	
Matched the student's developmental level:	

- Written, oral, or demonstrated, as appropriate to the students and the work.
- Individualized or group-directed, as appropriate to the students and the work.
- Focused on the work and the process the student used to do the work.
- Descriptive.
- Criterion-referenced (or, as appropriate, self-referenced).
- Positive.
- Clear.
- Specific.
- Supportive in tone.

Another way to recognize high-quality feedback is to look for its effects in the classroom. In classes where feedback is prominent,

- "Mistakes" are viewed as opportunities for learning.
- Students are not afraid to ask for help as needed.
- Assignments build on strengths and practice to overcome weaknesses. Feedback that students can't use because there is no further opportunity is not effective.
- Student self-efficacy is high.
- Students become better at appraising their own work.

Students learn from the models they have seen in their teacher's effective feedback to them. They learn self-assessment skills as they reproduce what their teachers have modeled, and they learn the value of review and revision and reshaping of work for improvement. "Getting it done" becomes less of a motivator than "figuring it out."

How Can I Model Effective Feedback in Conversations with Teachers About Their Own Professional Learning?

Your own feedback to teachers should follow the principles about strategies and content we have just described. Describe to teachers what you see in their practice. Identify their strengths. Even if you think a teacher knows what her strengths are, it is nice to have one's supervisor notice and name them. Then the teacher not only knows her strengths but also knows that you know. Here are some examples of ways to begin a conversation about feedback:

- *I know you return work to students in a timely manner, and I appreciate the amount of effort that takes. Let's look at some of the comments you make on student work and see if we can figure out a way for you to write less but be more effective.*
- *Next time we look together at one of your lessons, let's look at the whole cycle. Let's look at how your lesson plans, classroom activities and assignments, and feedback you gave tie together to advance your learning objectives.*
- *You have said that one of your main goals for students this year is for them to become more independent learners. Let's see how your feedback supports that goal.*
- *As you think about the fact that teacher feedback models for students how you want them to look at their work, what do you think are the most effective elements of your feedback? What parts of your feedback provide the most support for student growth?*

Feedback conversations about teachers' professional learning should in most cases be private, individual conversations. When weaknesses are identified, they should be treated as opportunities for development. The tone of the conversation should suggest to teachers that you believe they value improvement and are able to do it. Never identify a weakness without providing suggestions for what to do about it. If you, personally, do not have strategies to offer beyond what the teacher already has used, you can at least offer resources to help the teacher's development.

Finally, remember that your conversations are just that—conversations. Listen to a teacher's response to your feedback. If she is defensive, then she experienced your feedback as evaluation rather than description. Examine what you said and check to make sure it wasn't intended that way, and rephrase.

And this leads to our last point. Although supervisors, of course, should give feedback at the time of evaluations, these are primarily summative events. Teachers should receive formative feedback often, in situations not tied to evaluations, and while there is still time to improve before an evaluation.

What If?

Effective written feedback helps students learn. It's a genre of writing that may take time for teachers to develop, however. *What if you receive a call from a parent who says her child is receiving negative or insufficient feedback on assignments?*

First—and in keeping with the principles of good feedback—note what is positive about the call. Thank the parent for her interest and close attention to the work the student is taking home. Then ask what the specific concerns are.

Second, talk with the teacher. What was she trying to have the student accomplish—what was the learning target? Look at the work in question. Did the feedback match the learning target? Did it suggest at least one positive next step? Why does the parent think the feedback is negative or insufficient? It could be that the parent is looking for the kind of feedback she received in school—for example, expecting every usage error to be marked in red and interpreting no mark on a misspelled word to mean that the teacher didn't know or didn't care. You might suggest to the teacher that she schedule a meeting with the parent, and the student if appropriate, to discuss the work. A teacher-parent conference puts the communication where it needs to be and prevents a parental "end run" around the teacher.

If you notice that the feedback was, in fact, not of high quality in the sense that this chapter has described, you can also talk with the teacher about developing skills at providing effective feedback. The resources in this chapter, and others, can help you (Brookhart, 2008). As with any professional development, the best strategies are collaborative and inquiry-driven. You may be able to identify another teacher who can coach the teacher in improving feedback skills.

Reflecting on Feedback That Feeds Forward

Many teachers will say that "grading" takes up a lot of their time, and by that they may mean looking at student work whether it counts in the final grade or not. Encouraging teachers to give better feedback will be successful if you can demonstrate that less is more, that effective feedback really doesn't mean writing volumes, and that in the long run it will save time because it will help students improve their own learning. Reflect on the quality of feedback that you see in your school by asking these questions:

- Are there many instances of feedback on ungraded practice work? Or is most of the feedback that you see really an explanation of where students "lost points" in a grade?
- Can you identify classrooms in your school where the teacher uses feedback effectively, probably in conjunction with other formative assessment practices, in ways that she would be willing to share with colleagues? A demonstration of how targeted feedback supports learning and saves time in the long run might be helpful to other teachers.
- Are you leading by example? Do you give feedback to your teachers in ways that model the principles laid out in this chapter?

Summing It Up

In this chapter we have discussed feedback that does more than correct students' errors and instead informs their progress. Providing effective feedback is one of the most powerful things teachers can do to move students along in the learning process. The next chapter discusses student goal setting, one of the most powerful things *students* can do to move along in the learning process.

4

aCHIeVING MORe WITH FOCUS:
Fostering Student Goal Setting

It's no secret that students learn best when they are actively and intentionally engaged in their own learning. But classrooms full of actively engaged students don't just happen. They are created when teachers intentionally work to develop self-regulated learners who set their own goals, select effective strategies to reach those goals, and monitor and adjust what they do depending on the demands of the task and their own strengths and needs.

Although we recognize the enormous advantage that self-regulated learners enjoy in any learning situation, the reality is that few teachers use their day-to-day and minute-by-minute work in the classroom to help students learn how to learn. In too many classrooms, students are making poor decisions about what they should do, do next, or stop doing in order to improve. As a result, many students lack both the skill and the will to harness the workings of their own minds in order to succeed.

This chapter examines goal setting, a critical element of the formative assessment process, and explores ways that school leaders can encourage teachers to value and include skill development in goal setting as an integral part of their classroom practice. We also explore how goal setting can encourage teacher professional development and create a culture of collaborative inquiry in the school.

What Is Goal Setting?

> "Would you tell me, please, which way I ought to go from here?" asked Alice.
>
> "That depends a great deal on where you want to get to," said the Cheshire Cat.
>
> —Lewis Carroll, *Alice in Wonderland*

Goal setting is a critical element of the formative assessment process, a process guided by three core questions: *Where am I going? Where am I now? What strategy or strategies will help me get to where I need to go?* When students set a goal and then create and monitor a realistic plan to achieve it, they are engaged in their own learning in real and relevant ways.

A goal is what the student is trying to learn or achieve—an outcome or accomplishment. Achieving that goal in a realistic and strategic way is aided by goal setting, a cognitive process that effectively energizes a student to become more productive (Locke & Latham, 2002). Goal setting and goal achievement influence learning and generate motivation to learn in two important ways: first, by providing a learning target that students can see and understand; and second, by helping students gather information about how they are doing in pursuit of that target.

How Does Goal Setting Affect Student Learning and Achievement?

High-achieving students know what is important to learn and how to learn it. They tend to self-regulate more automatically than low-achieving students because they have "learned how to learn." These students set goals and then monitor their progress toward them. They assess the effectiveness of the strategies they chose for a particular learning task and then adjust the strategies accordingly to increase their probability of success. In fact, students who have internalized these important principles of learning—those who set goals and monitor their self-efficacy in this way—boost their achievement potential by as much as 30 percent (Zimmerman, 1998).

The formative assessment process boosts student achievement through its consistent and continuous focus on helping students learn how to learn. It weaves student goal setting into the day-to-day, minute-by-minute fabric of classroom life and strengthens the learning partnership between students and their teacher. By encouraging goal setting, formative assessment engages teachers in thinking about what the important concepts are and guides them as they make split-second decisions about how to best teach those concepts, mindful of what their students currently know and understand. And goal setting helps students focus on the important parts of the learning task as they make decisions about what to pay attention to, how to monitor their thinking, which strategy to select, and how to direct their effort in order to succeed. Goal setting helps everyone in the classroom learn how to learn.

In particular, goal setting helps students learn how to learn in four main ways (Locke & Latham, 1990):

1. *Goals focus student attention on the learning task and the learning target.* Students who set goals tied to the learning target focus on what is important and essential to success and are less likely to be pulled off course.
2. *Goals stimulate appropriate student effort.* Students learn to judge the degree and type of effort they will need to accomplish their goals, expending more effort to reach a more challenging goal.
3. *Goals increase student persistence.* With a clear and realistic goal in mind, students are more likely to attempt a challenging task, and should they fall short, they are more likely to choose a more effective strategy and try again.
4. *Goals increase a student's desire and capacity to learn new strategies.* Students who monitor their progress toward their goals look for and try new strategies that will help them more effectively reach their goals.

These four main influences have their greatest effect on student achievement when teachers help students set goals that are "just right" in terms of specificity, challenge, and probability for success (Pintrich & Schunk, 2002; Stipek, 2002). To promote student achievement, goal setting must be part of the daily life of the classroom, taught across the content areas, and continuously refined.

What Common Misconceptions Might Teachers Hold About Goal Setting?

There are three common misconceptions about goal setting that could dilute the quality of the formative assessment process. School leaders should use strategic talking points to counteract these misunderstandings and communicate accurate information about goal setting from the start.

Misconception #1: It is important that students have goals that inspire them to achieve more. Teachers commonly confuse a general, distant goal or personal wish with the kind of strategic goal setting that is integral to the formative assessment process. Or they conclude that any reasonable academic goal will do. Although it is inspiring for students to imagine their preferred futures (e.g., *I will grow up to play for the Steelers; I will work hard, save my money, and pay my own way on the field trip; I will get good grades so that my parents will buy me a puppy*), this is not the type of goal setting to which we refer. The power of the goals students learn to set during formative assessment derives from the goals being specifically focused on the learning task before the students and promoting inquiry into how the students can learn more effectively.

Strategic talking points school leaders can use to address this misconception include the following:

- Effective goal setting is a continuous process of learning how to learn.
- Effective goals are precise, detailed, and linked to the current classroom task, not to general academic aims.

Misconception #2: Goal setting is a planned event to help students prepare for the next unit, report period, or part of the school year. Teachers often think of goal setting as a periodic event rather than a continuous part of the learning process. They mistakenly view goal setting as something teachers and students do at the beginning of a school year, unit, or report card period, a time set aside to help students describe their aspirations for the weeks or months to come (e.g., *I will spend more time on my homework this nine weeks; I will raise my grade in English composition by setting aside more time to edit my work; I will come to class prepared to learn because I will read the chapters in the book and answer the end-of-chapter questions*). Although these general academic aims can inspire, they will not have the effect on student learning that comes from continuously setting detailed goals linked to the gap between precise learning targets and the student's current level of performance.

Strategic talking points school leaders can use to address this misconception include the following:

- Goal setting is an ongoing and continuous part of the formative assessment process.
- Teachers and their students use the goal-setting process to constantly inform their learning decisions in the classroom.

Misconception #3: Goal setting is a study skill. Many teachers see goal setting as a study skill rather than an integral part of the learning process in the classroom. To meet the criteria of formative assessment, goal setting must be a consistent part of how students learn, part of their ongoing efforts to gather information about their learning; and it should inform and be informed by their current skill and understanding relative to the task at hand. What is particularly dangerous about viewing goal setting as a study skill is that many middle school and high school teachers assume it is not their job to teach study skills as part of what they do in their classrooms, arguing that their focus should be on helping their students learn important course content.

Strategic talking points school leaders can use to address this misconception include the following:

- Goal setting is a learning process that helps students learn how to learn during the day-to-day, minute-by-minute work of the classroom.
- Students of all ages and in all grades learn more effectively and construct conceptual understandings in more meaningful ways when they take ownership of their learning through the goal-setting process.

What Is the Motivation Connection?

Goal setting generates motivation to learn by focusing students' attention on the gap between where they are and where they are heading. Knowing the distance between where you are and where you want to be and *can* be is a fundamental motivational principle (Locke & Latham, 2002). The three main phases of goal setting—setting the goal, selecting the strategy, and assessing performance—keep students "metacognitively, motivationally, and actively . . . engaged in their own learning process" (Zimmerman, 2001, p. 5). Simply put, goal setting keeps learners motivated to learn. And although a just-right goal can foster motivation to learn, being able to set a goal that is spot-on in terms of challenge, timing, and specificity is not a skill students acquire at birth. Goal setting must be taught and, like any skill set, requires scaffolding and opportunities for guided practice. Keeping this in mind, let's walk through the three main phases of goal setting, noting how the essential elements of the formative assessment process are critical to student success and how teachers work in partnership with their students to share information and gather crucial evidence.

Phase 1: Setting the Goal

During the first phase, *setting the goal*, students learn to describe a specific short-term learning goal that is just right in terms of challenge and attainment. Without a clear understanding of the learning target and the criteria for success, however, setting a goal that's accurate can be overwhelming for students. If students cannot distinguish the bite-sized chunks within a learning target, they will be unable to recognize logical and realistic steps they can take to ensure success. Helping students learn to set a goal that is just right requires much more than merely helping them state what they intend to do and how they will do it. A just-right short-term goal must be the logical next step students should take to close the gap between where they are and where they need to be. Determining that goal means students must make realistic estimates of their capacity to reach it. For example, let's consider a lesson focused on describing the characteristics of the planets. The first and perhaps most important step a teacher can take to encourage just-right goal setting is to help students identify the specific characteristics of the planets they should master. In our example, the characteristics could be the following: the distance of each planet from the sun, the relative size of the planets in relation to the size of the Earth, the characteristics of the "inner planets" versus the "outer planets," how long in Earth time it takes for each planet to revolve around the sun, and how long in Earth time it takes for each planet to rotate on its axis. Armed with this clear understanding of exactly what the teacher means by "characteristics," students can begin to gauge what they already know and what they need to learn. This act of realistically judging one's own ability (e.g., *I already know lots of things about the planets; I can already name the major planets and their distance from the sun*) and setting a goal to match it promotes self-efficacy.

What's more, just-right goals are neither too challenging nor too easily accomplished and are based on a clear understanding of the level of challenge, the time frame, and the learning sequence. They are a perfect fit because they describe accomplishments that are just slightly ahead of what a student can do now and aim at destinations the student can reach in the near future (Bandura & Cervone, 1986; Locke, 2002). In fact, specific and reasonably difficult goals lead to better performance than general "do your best" goals because they stimulate effort and help students to regulate their own actions. That is why the first phase, *setting the goal*, must involve students in examining the specific bite-sized chunks that make up the goal, the time frame they have to learn those chunks, and what they will be asked to do or produce at the end of that time frame to demonstrate their learning. It is critical, therefore, that teachers share as much information as possible about the specific learning targets and the criteria for success and provide ample time for students to examine the targets (review the detailed information in Chapter 2). For instance, if students realize that they have a week to learn the order, size, and distance from the sun of the planets and that they will be asked to draw a diagram of the planets at the end of the week, they can set goals for both learning about the planets and succeeding at the assignment—their goals become more specific and time bound.

Armed with specifics, each student has the opportunity to create a sequence of short-term, realistic goals that build on each other (e.g., *I already know Jupiter is the biggest planet, so now I need to learn the relative sizes of the rest of the planets and where they are in relation to the sun. Even though I am not great at drawing, I can use my compass to draw circles to represent the size of each planet in order to create my diagram, making sure each planet is the right size and in the right order from the sun*). And as students work through the week, the teacher provides feedback to feed them forward as they continually hone in on the difference between where they are and where they need to be.

Setting a just-right goal helps students work smarter and stay engaged (see Figure 4.1). It is a way to help students harness the workings of their own minds, set their own course, and monitor their progress toward the goal. And a goal that is on target works as a catalyst, helping students to channel their effort by focusing on what works and using appropriate levels of energy.

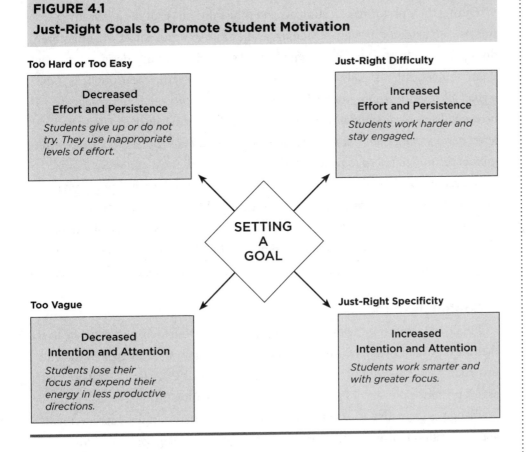

FIGURE 4.1
Just-Right Goals to Promote Student Motivation

Too Hard or Too Easy

Decreased
Effort and Persistence

Students give up or do not try. They use inappropriate levels of effort.

Just-Right Difficulty

Increased
Effort and Persistence

Students work harder and stay engaged.

SETTING A GOAL

Too Vague

Decreased
Intention and Attention

Students lose their focus and expend their energy in less productive directions.

Just-Right Specificity

Increased
Intention and Attention

Students work smarter and with greater focus.

Phase 2: Selecting the Strategy

After setting a goal, students enter the second phase of goal setting, *selecting a powerful set of strategies.* Armed with a specific and realistic short-term goal to guide them, students use their judgment to choose a strategy or set of strategies with "power"—a strategy they predict will have the most power to help them advance toward their goal (e.g., *I can use the 3-D model of the planets to help me compare their sizes; and in my learning group, I can get help with the idea of outer and inner planets*). And as students are planning and using specific strategies, they are benefitting from feedback and scaffolds as they work together with their teacher and peers.

Phase 3: Assessing Performance

During their performance, students enter the third phase of the goal-setting process, *self-assessing and self-regulating*, as they monitor and adjust what they are doing. Because they are equipped with a set of strategies carefully designed to help them, students intentionally and actively work to improve their learning (e.g., *I did a good job in my learning group when we quizzed each other on the inner planets because I knew the inner planets were smaller, were made mostly of rock, and had fewer or no moons. I am still not sure about how long it takes for each planet to revolve around the sun, so I need to read that part of the textbook again and make a chart to help me study*). Learning to gauge their progress toward their goal puts students in control of their own learning and means that students learn to attribute their success on the task at hand to things they can control—the set of strategies they choose and the amount and direction of their effort. They learn to gather evidence to assess the effectiveness of the strategies and to adjust their own performance.

A Continuous Process

Finally, students use the evidence they gathered during their performance to set their next goal accordingly. And the process begins again with a newly designed just-right goal. This continuous process of setting a goal, choosing a strategy, and assessing performance, all focused on improving learning during the task at hand, is what gives formative goal setting its power for increasing student achievement and motivation to learn. And when teachers consistently engage their students in understanding the learning targets and provide them with formative feedback along the way, students have the precise information they need to set specific, time-bound, and realistic short-term goals that are just right.

Clearly, many motivational benefits occur when students are actively and intentionally engaged in making informed learning decisions that help them move toward the learning target. Goal setting empowers students because it not only guides their journey but also helps them recognize and monitor their learning progress along the way. Because students are intimately involved in keeping track of where they are compared with where they want to be, they are better able to understand everyday setbacks as a natural part of learning. A teacher we work with in a school in western Pennsylvania helps her students understand the realities of tackling challenging learning tasks by talking to them about football.

Comparing her students to quarterbacks, she tells them to hang in there even after a setback. She explains that even Ben Roethlisberger, quarterback for the Pittsburgh Steelers, does not always reach the goal line on his first attempt. But like Big Ben, they should assess the distance between where they are and where they want to be in order to decide which strategy they should use next to keep their drive to the goal line alive and moving.

As the examples illustrate, teachers can find many ways to make goal setting a consistent and continuous part of what happens in the classroom. And when teachers help students see everyday connections between setting goals and choosing strategies with the best chance of helping them reach those goals, they maximize the motivational benefits goal setting can have for all students.

What Are Specific Strategies I Can Share with Teachers?

Learning to set goals takes time and practice. Teachers can use three strategies to promote goal setting: (1) using feedback that feeds forward, (2) modeling goal setting, and (3) providing goal-setting guides.

Using Feedback That Feeds Forward

The right kind of feedback (see Chapter 3) makes goal-directed behavior emotionally important for students. Effective feedback helps students judge their current level of performance. When teachers provide information that tells students that they are performing below the learning target, it causes dissatisfaction and negative emotions. On the other hand, information that students are performing at or above the learning target promotes positive emotions. It is critical for teacher feedback to include specific suggestions for what to do next.

By using feedback to feed forward, the teacher can increase learning no matter where the student is in relation to the goal. If the student is performing below goal level, specific suggestions can help the student set a just-right short-term learning goal that generates the motivation not only to work harder but also to tackle the learning task in a more strategic way. And when teacher feedback helps the student to see that he is making progress toward the learning target and provides suggestions for next steps, it encourages the student to set new short-term goals that are more challenging and that promote effort and persistence.

Modeling Goal Setting

When teachers model goal setting and allow students to become goal-setting models for each other, they help each student develop the skill and the will to learn more and learn smarter. Teachers can unpack the goal-setting phases and walk their students through goal setting as a consistent part of how they communicate with their students. Talking about learning in goal-directed language not only models goal setting but also helps to embed goal setting into the very fabric of specific learning tasks. Figure 4.2 summarizes the phases and steps of modeling goal setting and provides some sample language for teachers to use.

Providing Goal-Setting Guides

Goal-setting guides are a good way to help students internalize and visualize how to set goals and regulate their performance in a realistic and strategic way. Teachers can adjust the language to make it appropriate for their students' age and ability. Figures 4.3, 4.4, and 4.5 show several useful formats.

How Will I Recognize Goal Setting When I See It?

To be effective, goal setting must be part of everything that happens in the classroom, so look for evidence that goal setting is a process and not an event. Look for charts or posters that remind students of the importance of having goals or that list and describe goal-setting steps. Look for displays of student goal sheets or charts where students record their progress. Listen for teachers using goal-directed language in their conversations with their class or with individual students. Look and listen for students discussing their goals and their progress toward them with their peers.

Because goal setting is an ongoing process and not an event, you may not be able to observe it directly. However, you should be able to notice the following effects on the teacher:

- Lesson plans reflect intentions to include goal setting within the lesson.
- Assignments follow a logical sequence that scaffolds learners and breaks complex tasks into doable parts.
- Lessons include frequent progress checks for students to gauge their learning.

FIGURE 4.2
Modeling Goal Setting Through Goal-Directed Language

Goal-Setting Phases	Specific Steps *Help the students . . .*	What the Teacher Might Say
1. Set the Goal	• Recognize the learning goal.	*This week we will learn about the nine parts of the human eye.*
	• Clarify the level of challenge.	*We will learn all nine parts, not just some of them.*
	• Identify the specific bite-sized chunks that make the goal realistic and achievable and against which students will gauge their progress.	*There are many things to learn about the eye, but we are going to concentrate on learning to pronounce the name of each part, locate it, and describe what it does to help us see.*
	• Draw their attention to the learning time frame and how at the end of the time frame they will be asked to demonstrate their learning.	*On Friday, I will ask you to identify the parts of the eye on a drawing and write a statement about what each part does. This will help you judge where you are in learning the nine parts of the human eye.*
2. Select a Powerful Set of Learning Strategies	• Identify and use appropriate information resources.	*Let's think about the resources we can use to meet our goal. Our textbook has information and pictures. We can use the 3-D model and books in our class library. Our school library has interactive CD-ROMs, and we can use the Internet to link to Web sites that will help.*
	• Pinpoint strategies for meaningful collaborative learning.	*We will use class time each day to work in our learning groups. In your groups you can discuss each new part to make sure each person can identify and explain it. You can quiz each other and help each other recognize what you already know and what you need to learn.*

FIGURE 4.2
Modeling Goal Setting Through Goal-Directed Language *(cont.)*

Goal-Setting Phases	Specific Steps *Help the students . . .*	What the Teacher Might Say
2. Select a Powerful Set of Learning Strategies *(continued)*	• Prepare to use their time strategically.	*You have four days to learn the parts of the eye. By Wednesday you should know at least four parts, and by Friday you should know them all.*
3. Self-Assess and Self-Regulate	• Create a plan to assess their learning all along the way.	*Each day you will check where you are by using a checklist to identify the parts you know.*
	• Ask strategic questions to identify the just-right next step.	*Ask yourself: Where am I now? What should I do next?*
	• Uncover roadblocks and design specific ways to overcome them.	*What is confusing for you? What roadblocks are in your way? What can you do to overcome those roadblocks?*
	• Monitor which learning strategies are working well and which should be adjusted or changed (self-regulate).	*Think about the strategy or strategies you have used so far. What is working for you? What isn't? What should you keep on doing? What should you do differently or instead? Talk it over with your learning partner.*
4. Set the Next Goal	• Envision the next learning goal.	*Now that we can locate and explain the functions of the parts of the eye, we can work toward understanding how to protect our eyes from injury and disease. We will talk more about that on Monday.*

FIGURE 4.3
Sample Goal-Setting Guide

My Goal
This is my goal:
I will be able to reach my goal because I am good at doing these things:
I need to work on these:
I can count on these people to help me:
This is exactly what I am going to do:
This is how I will check my progress along the way:
This is when I plan to reach my goal:
This goal is important to me for these reasons:

FIGURE 4.4
Sample Goal-Setting Guide with To-Do List

My Learning Goal
Directions: Use this goal-setting guide to precisely state an important learning goal that you have for this lesson.
This is my goal:
The goal is important to me for the following reasons:
This to-do list will help me take action to reach my goal: ❏ ❏ ❏
My goal is both realistic and challenging for these reasons:
These will be the benefits of reaching my goal:
If I don't reach my goal, I could face these consequences:
These are the people I can count on to help me reach my goal:

FIGURE 4.5
Goal-Setting Organizer

My Goal-Setting Organizer: 5 *W*s and an *H*
What is my goal?
Where will I work on my goal?
Who will help me reach my goal?
Why is this goal important to me?
When will I reach my goal?
How will I reach my goal using these steps?

- Timelines for learning seem reasonable and practical.
- Students are encouraged to revise and resubmit assignments.

You should also be able to notice that students

- Are better at talking about where they are and where they are headed in relation to the learning task.
- Talk about where they are headed in terms of learning rather than aiming for certain grades.
- Seem more independent and self-assured.
- Revise and refine their work.

How Can I Model Goal Setting in My Conversations with Teachers About Their Own Professional Learning?

Goal setting is not just a good idea for students. It is also an indicator of teacher quality. You can use goal setting to help make teachers more aware of the strong link between the quality of their teaching and the learning progress that their students make.

Mirroring the importance of helping students learn to set and monitor goals that are directly related to specific classroom learning targets, you should help teachers set goals that are specifically focused on daily student learning (e.g., *I will help my students understand the relationship between asking questions and trying to come up with answers, and the scientific method*) rather than on professional goals (e.g., *I will complete my master's degree in the next two years*).

After observing a lesson, completing a walk-through, or having a discussion with a teacher, you can help the teacher visualize and set a specific goal that is directly related to specific classroom learning targets. The following strategic conversation starters will help move the teacher toward setting specific goals to influence student achievement.

- *Think with me for a minute about where your students are in relation to your specific learning targets, and let's talk about the daily evidence you are using to gauge students' academic achievement in relation to the specific targets.*
- *Let's talk a bit about the kinds of learning evidence you are collecting and what the evidence tells you about the gap between where your students are and where they are headed.*
- *Thinking about what we just discussed and envisioning tomorrow's lessons, let's talk about your specific goals for designing and adjusting your instruction in ways that will close the gap between where your students are performing and what that performance needs to look like in order to hit your learning target. Also, let's brainstorm ways can you provide each student the opportunity to benefit from goal setting.*
- *Now that you have specific goals in mind for your own teaching and strategies for helping your students set goals, let's talk about the kinds of resources that might help you and your students reach your goals.*

Notice that the sequencing of the conversation starters encourages teacher reflection, data-driven decision making, and specific goal setting related to student achievement. It helps teachers think in goal-directed ways about the specific content, learning activities, and reasoning process that will directly influence their students' learning.

What If?

Many teachers are already using contracts or goal-setting frameworks with their students. *What if you observe a teacher distributing goal sheets to students that give them their goals for the week?*

First, recognize the intention of the teacher to help students see where they are and what they need to do next. Then make clear the distinction between having a goal set for you and setting your own goal. Formative assessment helps students self-regulate and see themselves as competent learners. That means they might struggle with goal setting at first, but they will profit from seeing themselves as being in charge of their own learning.

Second, help the teacher see that goal setting is something effective students do regardless of their age or level of competence with a topic. Many teachers believe that younger students or students with learning challenges cannot set their own goals. Explain that with time to examine and understand the learning target and with scaffolding through effective feedback, the majority of students can learn to set appropriate goals for themselves. Help the teacher think about what scaffolds students would need to be successful and think through the roadblocks they imagine might limit students' success. For instance, help the teacher think about the degree to which students understand the essential parts of the learning target. Introduce the goal-directed language strategy. Talk about the importance of students having exemplars of excellent work before they begin a task.

Teachers must believe that all students are capable of learning to set goals. Helping them examine ways to teach and provide support for goal setting can help even the most fervent naysayers.

Reflecting on Fostering Student Goal Setting

Although we readily acknowledge the power of goals in our own lives, they remain the single most underestimated and underused means of improving student learning minute by minute and day to day in the classroom. Helping students learn the value of setting their own goals and regulating their own learning has powerful effects on their present and future achievement. Learning to tap into the power of goal setting helps all students become good students.

As you reflect on goal setting as an essential element in the formative assessment process, consider the following questions:

- Do teachers get the most leverage from the formative assessment process by combining student goal setting and feedback that feeds forward— that is, feedback that provides students with valuable insights into their progress and informs their thinking during goal setting?
- Do teachers provide students with direct instruction on the goal-setting process? Do they take the time to help students understand the learning targets and criteria for success by examining exemplars of excellent work to increase the probability that students will be able to set just-right goals?
- Do you encourage teachers to set and monitor their own professional goals? Do you dedicate time in faculty meetings to talk about the importance of setting and monitoring professional goals for making formative assessment a consistent part of what happens minute by minute and day to day in the classroom?

Summing It Up

Goal setting is a continuous process of learning how to learn. It is guided by clear learning targets and fueled by feedback that feeds forward. Teaching students to set just-right goals helps them know precisely what they want to achieve so they can choose powerful strategies and make informed decisions about how and where to concentrate their learning efforts.

But being a goal-setter is only one part of becoming an informed learner. Chapter 5 explores ways to move students beyond simply being skillful goal-setters to becoming actively involved goal-*getters*. These students know how to self-assess and make learning decisions based on the information they gather in order to direct and regulate their own learning.

5

HELPING GOAL-SETTERS BECOME ACTIVE GOAL-GETTERS:
The Role of Student Self-Assessment

Assessing one's own work results in increased learning; assessing a peer's work does not. Sadler and Good (2006) trained students to use rubrics to grade tests in their middle school science classes. Students who graded their own tests improved dramatically on a second, unannounced administration of the same test, whereas students who graded peers' tests did not gain significantly more on the second test than did a control group of students who did no grading at all.

Student self-assessment is not something that comes naturally to many. If you just ask students whether they understand something, many will say either "yes" (whether they do understand or not) or "I have no clue." Students can be taught, however, to use criteria to assess their work and then interpret what that self-assessment means for their next steps. The teacher needs to be skilled not only at teaching a skill (self-assessment) but also at interpreting student progress. Teachers who understand learning progressions with the material in question—how students typically do with this learning goal, how understanding typically develops, and what meaningful ways there are to chunk the task into smaller bites, if needed—will be better facilitators of student self-assessment than those who don't.

Remember that in Chapter 3 we said this same thing about giving feedback. Teacher feedback to students and student self-assessment are related activities. Both should compare student work against criteria for successful achievement of a learning target. Both should lead to the student knowing some next steps for improvement. Teacher feedback does these things from the expert point of view, and student self-assessment does these things from the learner point of view.

What Is Student Self-Assessment?

Student self-assessment, as we are using the term here, occurs when students review their own work and identify strengths and weaknesses for the purpose of improving performance. Students self-assess when they compare their work against their own conception of what they were trying to accomplish. Students identify their own strengths and weaknesses, decide how they are progressing on their way to a goal, and decide what they think they should do next.

Whether we should have considered student self-assessment before or after student goal setting is a chicken-and-egg matter. Sometimes students set goals and then monitor their progress toward them with self-assessment—the approach we took in this book by making goal setting the topic of Chapter 4 and self-assessment the topic of Chapter 5. However, the process is cyclical. Sometimes students assess their own work and then, as a result, decide to set a goal.

How Does Student Self-Assessment Affect Student Learning and Achievement?

Student self-assessment offers students an opportunity to review their work and become more aware of their strengths, their progress, and the gaps in learning that still need to be addressed. Sometimes teachers use student self-assessment as a time-saver for grading tests. Although this chapter is about self-assessment for formative purposes, not grading, the Sadler and Good (2006) study we mentioned at the start of the chapter is worth reporting here. Students who graded their own science tests benefited, scoring higher on a second administration of the same test. Students who graded a peer's science test did not increase their achievement on the same test (Sadler & Good, 2006). In addition, in later reflection some students were able to voice the opinion that grading their own tests gave them a more positive attitude toward tests as providing useful feedback.

Self-assessment of the sort we are concerned with here is usually *not* for grading. It is a process that students do as part of their learning activities. To self-assess well, students need a clear concept of the learning goals and criteria, skill at recognizing these characteristics in their own work when they see them, and skill at translating their self-assessment judgments into action plans for improvement. These are skills that can, and should, be taught. Ross, Hogaboam-Gray, and Rolheiser (2002) found that 5th and 6th graders who received 12 weeks of self-evaluation training in mathematics increased mathematics problem-solving achievement, with an effect size (standardized difference) of .40 standard deviations, or the equivalent of moving from the 50th percentile to the 66th percentile on a standardized test.

Another study looked at the effects of reading a model writing assignment, generating a list of criteria for the assignment, and self-assessing according to a rubric for 3rd and 4th graders' family stories or persuasive essays. Students who participated in these activities wrote better stories and essays than students who simply generated a list of criteria and then were asked to review their first drafts (Andrade, Du, & Wang, 2008). The difference seemed to be systematic self-assessment using the criteria in the rubric. Just looking over the first draft was not enough.

What Common Misconceptions Might Teachers Hold About Student Self-Assessment?

Teachers are likely to hold at least one common misconception about student self-assessment.

Misconception #1: Student self-assessment means students grade their own work. The most common misconception teachers might hold about student self-assessment isn't really a misconception at all but, rather, a misuse of the strategy. The misconception is, of course, that student self-assessment means students grading their own work. The kind of self-assessment we hold up as formative involves students reviewing their own work with an eye toward learning (a formative purpose), not grading (a summative purpose). Although students can learn from grading their own work, that is not what we are recommending. Rather, we recommend that students routinely and systematically have the opportunity to look at their work and plan for improvement.

Strategic talking points school leaders can use to address this misconception include the following:

- Students need—and deserve—opportunities to practice with concepts and skills before they are graded. In a classroom instructional sequence, formative assessment fits better as part of practice than of graded assignments, where the concepts and skills should have been mastered already.
- Students will be able to focus on the substance of the work if they are free of the need to focus on what their grade is.

What Is the Motivation Connection?

Many teachers are familiar with the concept called "self-efficacy," a student's perception that she can learn particular content or skills and will be successful in doing so. Self-evaluation contributes to self-efficacy, because it gives students a means by which they can accomplish goals by observing and interpreting their own performance. As the research indicates, "Students with greater confidence in their ability to accomplish the target task are more likely to visualize success than failure" (Ross et al., 2002, p. 45).

Self-assessment also helps students become self-regulated learners. Self-regulation is broader than self-efficacy. Most self-regulated learners do have self-efficacy, but they also have a habit of making sure they attend to their learning progress. They check to make sure they understand what they are supposed to do, plan and monitor their own work as they do it, assess their own progress, know when they need to ask questions, and give themselves their own internal rewards for achievement. They are actively engaged in collecting and interpreting assessment information. Information about their own progress helps them set more realistic and attainable goals for continuously raising achievement.

When teachers use formative assessment strategies well, they model for students how to do these things. Students gradually internalize the process. Self-regulation strategies can be taught, and they can be scaffolded for students who have difficulty learning them.

What Are Specific Strategies I Can Share with Teachers?

The first strategy to share is about when *not* to ask students to self-assess. At the very beginning of studying a new concept or learning a new skill, when students' vision of the learning target is not well developed, teacher feedback takes precedence. Good teacher feedback models for students how to observe their work and how to evaluate it against criteria.

Once students have had some experience with a learning target, they are in a position to understand the criteria for good work more deeply—or even to develop a list of those criteria themselves—and to apply them thoughtfully. Figure 5.1 summarizes the strategies that we discuss in the following sections.

Teaching Self-Assessment

To teach students self-assessment skills, the teacher should work with a learning target students already know something about. First, the teacher can involve students in developing their own criteria. This doesn't mean that students invent new criteria. Students who already know something about math problem solving (Ross et al., 2002), for example, or about writing (Andrade et al., 2008) usually come up with fairly typical lists when asked to generate a list of the important qualities of that kind of work. The main point is that they came up with these criteria themselves instead of receiving them from the teacher. Involvement is built in. The students must actively process what they know about the learning target—good problem solving, good writing, and so on—in order to do this.

The criteria are then "in mind," and students' review of their work can be "mindful." Students' first attempts at self-assessment may be too vague to be useful or may not focus on all relevant characteristics of the work. Teachers should give students timely, descriptive feedback on their self-assessments. They should ask students questions to clarify their thinking. For example, a teacher might use follow-up prompts like "Why?" or "Explain that" or "Tell me more about . . ." for both oral and written student self-assessment comments.

Teachers should also give students criteria for the actual self-assessment reflections. For example, a teacher of younger students might say that each reflection should include at least one sentence about a thought or feeling and at

---

FIGURE 5.1
Strategies for Student Self-Assessment

General Strategy	Specific Tactics
Teaching Self-Assessment	• Students develop their own criteria or rubrics or are given criteria or rubrics by the teacher. • Students use criteria or rubrics to assess their own work. • Teachers give students feedback on the quality of their self-assessments. • Teachers give students opportunities to practice self-assessment regularly.
Rubrics and Highlighters	• Students highlight portions of rubrics that they think apply to their work. • Teachers highlight portions of rubrics that apply to students' work.
Indicator Systems	• Students provide information about their understanding by using signals or response systems: – Happy/sad faces or red/green traffic lights – Letter cards (*A, B, C, D*) for multiple-choice questions – True/false or yes/no questions with physical movement – Individual whiteboards – "Most clear" and "least clear" cards
Self-Assessment Before and After Tests	• Students generate practice test questions and use them for studying. • Students plan study for a test by evaluating what they understand and what they don't understand. • Students assess their test results, looking for patterns in performance. • Students graph progress on repeated tests and reflect.
Self-Assessment of Effort	• Students judge levels of effort for an assignment, with separate considerations for time, concentration, and care. • Students assess their use of strategies after an assignment.

least one sentence telling why. More general criteria for student self-assessment might be that reflections should

- Be relevant.
- Be thoughtful.
- Be clearly expressed.
- Give reasons.
- Include a "so what" (what to do next to use the insights).

And finally, teachers should give students plenty of practice at self-assessment. Daily journals, exit tickets, or other opportunities for reflection should become routine.

Rubrics and Highlighters

When students self-assess their written work using rubrics, a helpful strategy is to have them use a highlighter to highlight key phrases in the rubric that they think describe their work and then use the same color highlighter to mark in their drafts the evidence that they have met the highlighted standard. For example, if a student highlighted "clearly states an opinion" in a rubric for a persuasive essay, that student would also highlight the opinion in the draft (Andrade et al., 2008). An important next step should follow for places where students find they need improvement. Students should write reminders for themselves about where they did not find a match between their work and the rubrics and use that information when revising their work. Although this example is about writing, a similar process can be used with rubrics for math problem solving, social studies and science projects, and other student work.

Chappuis (2005) describes a variation on this strategy. Students highlight in yellow the portions of a rubric they think describe their work and then turn the work in. The teacher highlights the same rubric in blue for each student. Where the colors overlap, indicating student-teacher agreement, the highlight will be green. Areas that are just yellow or just blue represent areas where students need to rethink their understanding of the criteria. Or they may be areas that could inspire productive conversations between teacher and student.

Indicator Systems

Self-assessment can be more immediate and less comprehensive than what is required for reviews of major pieces of work. Indicator systems can help students give teachers information about what they understand and don't understand, or where they get stuck doing an assignment. Teachers can use this information to affirm understanding and clarify misconceptions in a just-in-time fashion: students get the information just when they are thinking about it and need it.

Some formative assessment strategies using indicator systems have become fairly common. Here are some examples:

- **Happy/sad faces or red/green light cards** can help students indicate whether they are understanding a lesson as it progresses. Students can turn up the sad face or the red light side of the card when they feel stuck or need help.
- **Letter cards (*A, B, C, D*)** can be used to check understanding by having students hold them up to indicate their response to multiple-choice questions. Follow-ups can include calling on students (before the teacher gives the correct answer) to explain the reason for their choice or grouping students and having them try to convince others of the correctness of their answer.
- **True/false or yes/no questions** with answers indicated by raising a hand or some other kind of physical response (e.g., *Stand up if you think the cork will float*) is a variation of the letter-card strategy that works well with younger children.
- **Individual whiteboards** can be used for seeing how all students, not just a few who are called on, answer questions or problems. Students hold up their whiteboards so the teacher can see their responses.
- **"Most clear" and "least clear" cards** are a way for students to identify the most and least clear points after a lesson, using index cards or another easy-to-handle medium. The teacher collects the cards and uses the information to adjust instruction. Variations include asking students to identify "the sticking point" or "one thing I'm sure I know" or "one thing I'd like to know more about."

Indicator systems require that students assess their own understanding of what is happening in class. The effectiveness of an indicator system depends on both the quality of the students' self-assessment and the appropriateness of the teacher's responses. None of these systems work unless the information they generate is *used*. For example, it does a student no good to display a sad-face indicator unless the teacher notices this, talks with the student, and addresses the source of confusion. It is the use of the information that is formative, not the indicator itself.

Self-Assessment Before and After Tests

A variety of strategies can help students use information about their understanding and the quality of their work to set goals and to organize their studying.

Before a test is given, students can generate their own practice test questions. Teachers can give students the test blueprint (an outline of how many questions of various kinds and content will be on the test) and ask them to write at least one "fact" question and one "reasoning" question for each area. Students can share questions in class and use them for studying for the test. The act of writing the questions is itself an aid to comprehension. Phrasing the question will make students think about the concept.

Self-reflection sheets can include columns for planning how to study for a test. For example, students can make columns labeled "I get it" and "I don't get it." For Column 1 ("I get it"), they plan to review before the test; for Column 2 ("I don't get it"), they plan how they will learn the material. Homework sheets, home-help sheets, or logs can include, as appropriate, topic, time, place, helper (such as a parent or a friend), and resources (such as books or notes).

After a test, students can go over their own tests, noting which questions they got wrong and whether it was a careless error or a true misunderstanding. Students can use this information to plan future work. Strategies for addressing careless errors include taking more time and checking work. Strategies for addressing misunderstandings include reviewing notes, books, or other class materials and asking for help if the concept still isn't clear.

For repeated lessons, students can keep charts or graphs of progress or use other self-monitoring strategies and reflect on them. A very successful formative assessment effort in this regard happened in two 3rd grade classes and was, in fact, designed by a student teacher. She first called the strategy "GPAR" (for Goal, Plan, Action, Reflection), but we ended up calling it "Minute Math." The students were learning their multiplication facts. Each week for 10 weeks, they were to take a 100-fact timed test to see how many multiplication facts they could get right in five minutes. This, of course, is a rote-memory activity. The student teacher's strategy changed it into a higher-order activity that involved teaching students self-monitoring and self-regulation strategies. Students predicted how they would do and graphed their predictions on bar graphs (see Figure 5.2). After the test, they graphed their actual score and completed a reflection sheet (like the one in Figure 5.3) that included questions about their goal for the next week's test and their plan for achieving it. Student predictions were accurate, on average, and became more accurate with time, although there was great variability in accuracy.

Many students overpredicted their achievement for the first week and then became more accurate over time. Some students learned all the facts before the 10 weeks were over and decided that they would try to beat the clock, predicting, for example, that they could do the problems in four-and-a-half minutes the next week. A side effect that one of the 3rd grade teachers noticed was that she thought her students became better at making and interpreting bar graphs because of the Minute Math project.

The other 3rd grade teacher didn't like the GPAR reflection sheet in Figure 5.3, the one designed by her colleague's student teacher. This teacher made a version that was more like a worksheet and required less student writing and thinking—that is, less active student self-assessment. Although the project helped with student achievement in both classes (most students did reach 100 percent attainment of the learning goal), students in this second class did not do as well overall with their multiplication facts. The classroom environment was key. Genuine reflection was more supported in the first classroom. Getting the task accomplished—filling in the form easily and correctly—was more of the emphasis in the other classroom.

For the most part, students enjoyed participating in self-assessment. Students liked seeing their "steps," as they called their progress on the graphs. Student comments in the self-reflections indicated an orientation toward goal mastery. Student achievement was high (Brookhart, Andolina, Zuza, & Furman, 2004). This

FIGURE 5.2
"Minute Math" Student Tool

Prediction and Record Sheet

P = predicted score (yellow)
A = actual score (blue)

	P	A	P	A	P	A	P	A	P	A	P	A	P	A	P	A	P	A	P	A
100																				
95																				
90																				
85																				
80																				
75																				
70																				
65																				
60																				
55																				
50																				
45																				
40																				
35																				
30																				
25																				
20																				
15																				
10																				
5																				
0	P	A	P	A	P	A	P	A	P	A	P	A	P	A	P	A	P	A	P	A
Date																				
Test score																				
Student prediction																				

FIGURE 5.3
Reflection Sheet for "Minute Math"

Name _____ Date _____

GOAL: What do you want to learn?

_____

_____

_____

Right now I can do _____ facts in five minutes.

PLAN: My goal is to get ____ out of 100 facts correct on my next test. I need to improve in

_____

_____

_____

ACTION: When will you begin? Starting _____ I will use these study strategies to improve (study flash cards, play multiplication games, study with parents, etc.):

_____

_____

_____

RESULTS: Did you follow through with your plan? What happened? Did you see improvements?

_____

_____

_____

Minute Math strategy supported student self-assessment by surrounding it with scaffolding. The strategy required prediction (of the next week's score), reflection (on current and desired performance), goal setting, and strategy planning.

The bar graph itself became an important visual. In fact, one of the teachers thought she might use the bar graph by itself the following year, without the reflection sheet, although we think that would be a mistake because it would eliminate some opportunities for student self-reflection. This strategy could be adapted to any repeated assessment—for example, with vocabulary words, weekly lab reports, or any other routine and ongoing assessment.

Self-Assessment of Effort

Students can reflect on their individual effort. Teachers should try to have students assess different aspects of their effort. If a teacher just asks students how much effort an assignment required, most students will respond in terms of how much time it took them to complete. Teachers can avoid this response by asking students separate questions: *How much time did you spend? How hard did you concentrate? How carefully did you work? How did you handle new ideas or aspects of the assignment that you weren't sure how to do at first? How much help did you need, and did you ask for it?* And so on. Then, students can reflect—individually, with the teacher, or in small groups—about anything they learned that they will use in their next big project or assignment. Study strategies are a big part of self-regulation. It's not enough to know what steps to take for improvement; students need to know what to do to actually improve.

How Will I Recognize Effective Student Self-Assessment When I See It?

Effective student self-assessment is present when students can tell you about their strengths and weaknesses. Effective student self-assessment is present when students see the value of reflection and begin to do it routinely, whether asked to or not. Look for the following things to be happening in a classroom where effective student self-assessment is occurring:

- Students are asked to evaluate their own work regularly.
- Students set their own goals and monitor their progress toward them.

- Students can describe their own strengths and weaknesses.
- The classroom environment makes it safe for students to ask for help.
- Mistakes are seen as opportunities for learning.

How Can I Model Effective Self-Assessment in Conversations with Teachers About Their Own Professional Learning?

One thing you can do to encourage effective teacher self-assessment is to make it a safe activity. If admitting a need for help results in a supervisor rating a teacher poorly, the teacher will, of course, not feel able to do that.

Beyond providing a safe environment, you can encourage effective self-assessment among teachers by

- Communicating clearly the goals for professional learning.
- Having teachers generate the criteria for assessing progress on these goals.
- Agreeing on the criteria.
- Encouraging frequent reflection and communication.
- Responding to teacher self-assessment with supportive feedback.
- Following each supervisory visit with a conversation in which you ask the teacher what she thinks are her strengths and weaknesses.

You can also use the following conversation starters to help teachers assess and monitor their own classroom practices as they relate to promoting student self-assessment.

- *One of your strengths as a teacher is your belief in your students. I can see that as I observe your teaching. Tell me a little more about why you treat your students so respectfully and what that means for you.*
- *You have been working on student involvement in active learning all year. Let's talk about ways we can extend that student involvement into student assessment of their own work. What do you think they would need to be able to handle that?*
- *The rubrics you have been using for this project are really sound. Let's talk about ways you can have students use the rubrics, too—before, during, and after their work on the project.*

- *One of life's little mysteries is the fact that when teachers give over control of learning to their students, they don't have less control themselves over learning but in fact preside over a classroom environment that is more conducive to learning. Let's explore ways you can experiment with that in your classroom.*

What If?

Some school cultures are more conducive to student self-assessment than others. Sometimes individual teachers or whole schools have established an authoritarian climate that views appraisal of a student's work as "the teacher's job." Teachers who encourage student self-assessment may at first be accused, by students or their parents, of falling down on the job or abdicating their responsibilities. *What if you run into a parent or student who expresses this attitude?*

The strategic talking points in the section above on common misconceptions about student self-assessment are a good place to start. Many students and parents have been socialized into a view of schooling that sees grades as currency that students earn as they do little bits of work; and from that view it follows that it is the teacher who should be in charge of assessment, meting out the rewards. The problem with this view is that it doesn't really reflect how students learn. Whether a student or parent (or teacher, for that matter) likes it or not, students learn from active engagement with material and from figuring out their position relative to the material. What is it, and what do they know about it already? Is it of interest? Is it important? How much effort will they have to expend, and is the learning worth it? What will they have to do to achieve at the level they're aiming for or willing to accept? Even in an authoritarian climate, active and successful learners are asking these questions internally.

Given that reality, it isn't a matter of whether teachers are going to "let" students self-assess. It's a matter of whether teachers are going to harness this important tool equitably, teaching all students how to intentionally monitor their own understanding, giving all students this lifelong skill. And it certainly isn't a matter of abdicating responsibility. Teachers are responsible for structuring all the opportunities to learn in their classroom, and that includes opportunities for student self-assessment. There is plenty of teacher direction involved in planning the activities and tools—for example, constructing checklists and planning how students will use them—for student self-assessment. There is plenty of need for teachers' professional skills, too, as evidenced by the fact that we have seen as many poorly constructed, ineffective checklists as good ones!

So the school leader will have to lead some cultural change for this cause. It may involve explanations to parents who are looking for the same kind of schooling for their children as they experienced themselves. More powerfully, and more convincingly, it will involve showing students and parents how much more progress can be made when students actually look out for where they're going.

Reflecting on Student Self-Assessment

We recommend starting your reflection on student self-assessment by considering this statement about attitude: Student self-assessment can only flourish if the ground is prepared. Once a learning culture and student involvement put down firm roots, then look for models and strategies teachers can share among themselves.

Use the following questions to guide your reflection on student self-assessment:

- Which teachers and students in your school believe that student self-assessment, with students self-aware about what they know and can do, is essential for real learning? Are there some who do not believe this? How could you show them a different possibility?
- What are some self-assessment activities that work well for students and teachers in various grades and subject areas in your school?
- How can you facilitate helping teachers share these ideas?

Summing It Up

Taken together, student goal setting and student self-assessment (covered in Chapters 4 and 5 in this book) are the most effective means to empower students. Student goal setting and student self-assessment are self-regulation activities that put students in control of their own learning. *Every* student, no matter what age or developmental level, is an active learner. There is no such thing as "passive learning." School leaders should believe that. Teachers should avoid the trap of trying to "help" by giving passive prescriptions to poor students and assuming active self-assessment is only for good students. Either students are the captain of their own ship of learning or there is no ship—that is, no learning. Teachers should treat all students as if this were true, because it is.

6

ENRICHING CLASSROOM DISCOURSE:
Planning For and Asking Strategic Questions

> More effort has to be spent in framing questions that are worth asking: that is,
> questions that are critical to the development of student understanding.
>
> —Paul Black, Christine Harrison, Clare Lee, Bethan Marshall, & Dylan Wiliam,
> *Assessment for Learning: Putting It into Practice*

Consider this: An average teacher asks 400 questions each day, roughly 70,000 questions each year, or 2 to 3 million questions over a teaching career. That means teachers spend a third of their time asking questions. Yet most of the questions teachers pose are answered in less than a second—the average time teachers wait before accepting an answer, calling on someone else, or answering the question themselves (Hastings, 2003).

Sadly, in most schools teachers still dominate classroom talk, relying on a traditional initiate-respond-evaluate (IRE) structure for classroom discourse. The IRE structure creates an imbalance of power in which teachers are the only ones who initiate classroom talk, share information, ask questions, and give directions. And to the detriment of all that occurs in that classroom, the IRE format sends the loud and clear message that

- All interactions are teacher initiated.
- Students speak *only* when invited by the teacher.

- The teacher decides what knowledge is valuable (Cazden, 2001).
- The teacher determines the pace the lesson should follow (Dillon, 1988).
- Student responses are either right or wrong.

Embedded in the IRE structure, teachers rapidly move from one question to the next, rarely providing the kind of formative feedback that helps students assess the gap between where they are and where they need to be to reach the lesson's learning target.

In this chapter we examine the role teacher questions play in the formative assessment process. We also explore how strategic teacher questioning can promote meaningful classroom conversations.

What Is Strategic Teacher Questioning?

Strategic teacher questions—questions that promote formative discourse—share three characteristics: (1) they are planned for, (2) they help students harness the workings of their own minds, and (3) they use appropriate "wait time" to increase student accountability and the complexity of student responses. These skillful questions focus students' attention on content and concepts that are critical to the learning targets, build logically and directly on students' prior knowledge, stimulate students' reasoning in ways that help them formulate personal responses, and result in learning that is richer, deeper, and more integrated (Dillon, 1988; Walsh & Sattes, 2005).

Led by a skillful teacher employing strategic questioning, formative classroom discourse—whether it lasts five minutes or spans an entire class period—can provide a "safe place" where students can self-assess. During formative discussions, strategic questions can both "assist and assess student learning" (Cazden, 2001, p. 92). These skillful questions foster active student engagement with important concepts, content, and reasoning processes in the context of specific subject matter. And when teachers use effective questioning, they continuously direct students' focus to important learning targets, helping them to assess where they are, where they want to be, and what they have to do to get there.

When teachers plan for and ask strategic questions, they begin to systematically examine their classroom questioning patterns. Many teachers are unaware of the questioning ruts that influence what happens in their classrooms. Formative assessment not only can make those ruts visible but also can give teachers practical strategies for escaping them in order to raise the quality of the questions they ask and ensure equitable opportunities for all students to engage in meaningful discussion.

How Does Strategic Teacher Questioning Affect Student Learning and Achievement?

Teacher questioning is still the most common form of interaction between the student and the teacher in virtually every type of lesson across grade levels. Raising the quality of teacher questioning, therefore, can result in rapid and positive changes in the classroom that have a powerful effect on student learning and achievement (Clarke, 2005). Strategic teacher questions scaffold student learning and pull cognitive development. We can use the three characteristics of strategic teacher questioning (they are planned for, they help students harness the workings of their own minds, and they use appropriate wait time to increase student accountability and the complexity of student responses) to examine its effect on student learning.

Questions That Are Planned

Using strong evidence of student learning gathered day to day and minute by minute during the formative assessment process, classroom teachers take time to frame strategic questions that promote increasingly sophisticated conceptual understandings of the important content and reasoning processes tied to the lesson's learning targets. In their planning, teachers design questions that focus student attention on just-right next steps to take in thinking critically about the lesson's content. These questions tend to be "open" rather than "closed" and require responses that demonstrate the student's ability to think beyond factual recall or literal paraphrasing of content (see Figure 6.1).

Questions That Help Students Harness the Workings of Their Own Minds

Strategic teacher questioning, when done effectively, provides a medium for assessing learning that is immediate and accessible for both teachers and their students. When teachers frame and ask high-quality questions during

FIGURE 6.1
Closed Versus Open Questions

Closed Questions	Open Questions
• Imply there is only one predetermined "correct" answer. *What is the capital of Pennsylvania?*	• Invite a range of responses and make progressive demands on student thinking. *As you think about the state of Pennsylvania, why do you suppose its founders chose to locate the state capital in Harrisburg?*
• Almost always ask students to recall facts or to demonstrate simple comprehension. *What is a ratio?*	• Encourage students to think beyond the isolated facts to authentic and relevant uses of concepts. *Using the number of males and females in our class, how many ratios can you write?*
• Are designed to determine whether the student knows, understands, or can do a predetermined thing. *Can you name something that dissolves?*	• Are designed to increase and gauge the quality of what students know, understand, and can do as they make progress toward the learning target. *What rules about physical changes can we come up with to help us determine if something has melted or dissolved?*

formative discourse, they prompt students to inspect their existing knowledge and experience to create new understanding. And as teachers ask strategic questions, they model for their students how experienced learners seek clarity and, in doing so, scaffold their students in refining their abilities to self-assess and self-regulate.

Because many competencies take time to develop, students benefit from engaging in conversations that help them become aware of any gaps between their current competency levels and those required to reach the learning target. These benefits are not available to students who think and reason in isolation. Without exposure to formative discourse focused by strategic teacher questioning, many students mistakenly believe they have mastered certain concepts or reasoning processes, when in reality there are gaps between where they are and where they need to be. Thinking with others during focused formative discussions creates the potential for students to become much more aware of their actual level of knowledge so they can intentionally work toward developing more sophisticated conceptual understandings of important ideas and relationships related to targeted content and reasoning processes.

Here are some examples of strategic questions that prompt students to self-assess, to set goals, and to self-regulate during formative discourse:

- *How did you arrive at your conclusion about ways to save electricity in our school? Talk about what you did so that we can all check our thinking.*
- *What steps did you take to create a set of interview questions to ask Mr. Gabriel about why he decided to become a school superintendent? Did anyone use a different set of steps to come up with their interview questions?*
- *How did you decide how much time to plan for editing your essay before you handed it in? How will your decision help you reach your goals for your essay?*
- *As you observed the thermometer that we inserted into the mitten, what did you learn about the ways we currently misuse the terms* heat *and* temperature?
- *When you were trying to predict the probability of finding more red candies in your bag of candy than other colors, how did your understanding of fractions help you to make your predictions?*
- *What strategies did you use in putting together your leaf book that helped you to keep organized? If you had it to do again, what would you do differently? What would you do in the same way, and why?*
- *The idea that you just shared about the role that slaves played in the economy of the South is important, but general. Can you be more specific?*

Questions That Use Appropriate Wait Time

Strategic teacher questions use appropriate wait time to increase student accountability and raise the complexity of student responses. It takes time to think. Yet in her research, Mary Budd Rowe (1974) discovered that "wait time"—the period of silence that follows teacher questions and students' completed responses—rarely lasted more than one and a half seconds in typical classrooms, regardless of grade level or content. Encouraging teachers to extend wait time beyond the one and a half seconds that is currently the norm in most classrooms is a strategy that appears too simple to have a significant effect on student learning and achievement. However, when teachers wait in silence for three or more seconds after they pose an open, higher-order question, and after a student responds, many positive things happen for students and teachers (Rowe, 1986; Stahl, 1994; Tobin, 1987).

When students receive three or more seconds of undisturbed wait time and get used to higher expectations for their responses,

- Their responses increase in length and correctness.
- They give fewer "I don't know" and no-answer responses.
- Their self-efficacy increases.
- More students volunteer and give appropriate answers.
- More students challenge, expand upon, or add to the responses of other students.
- They offer an increased number of alternative responses.
- They increase the amount of student-to-student questioning.
- Their scores on academic achievement tests increase.

When teachers wait patiently in silence for three or more seconds after asking a question or hearing a student's response,

- Their questioning strategies tend to be more flexible and varied.
- They decrease the number of low-level, closed questions they ask.
- They increase the quality and variety of open, higher-order questions.
- They ask additional questions that require more thinking and reasoning.
- They more accurately gauge where their students are in relation to learning targets.
- They ask questions that focus on the logical next step students need to take to deepen understanding.

We explore specific wait-time strategies later in this chapter. Teachers can use these and other wait-time strategies after posing a strategic question in order to help students learn to think and reason with their classmates. When students talk with their peers about ideas, learning targets, and classroom work, they are engaging in conversations that are formative and fundamental to learning.

By signaling to students that they should wait, think, and discuss before they volunteer a response, teachers can promote high amounts of talk that is productive and directly related to the content and the reasoning processes being studied. During these discussions, teachers guide their students to focus on the subject matter, to use accurate facts and sources of information that are appropriate to the conversation's focus, to weigh and consider what their classmates have to say (Fisher & Frey, 2007), to challenge misconceptions and inaccuracies, and to be prepared to supply evidence for any claims they will make in their responses. In other words, formative discussions led by strategic questioning and supported by appropriate wait time go a long way toward promoting "accountable talk"— formative conversations that hold students accountable to each other, accountable for getting their facts and evidence right, and accountable for using rigorous thinking (Michaels, O'Conner, Hall, & Resnick, 2002).

What Common Misconceptions Might Teachers Hold About Strategic Questioning?

Teachers commonly hold three misconceptions about strategic questioning.

Misconception #1: The primary purpose for questioning students is to evaluate what they have learned. Teachers routinely think of questioning as a vehicle for establishing what students already know. During the formative assessment process, strategic questions do more than audit learning; they engage students in the kinds of thinking that further their learning. Questions that merely audit learning do not inform the learning or engage students in thinking and goal setting.

Strategic talking points school leaders can use to address this misconception include the following:

- Strategic questions help students think in new ways and further their learning.
- Strategic questions help students self-assess, set goals, and self-regulate.

Misconception #2: Asking good questions is something teachers can do naturally, "on the fly." Teachers assume that they routinely ask their students high-quality questions, and they see little need to plan for and frame strategic questions as a consistent part of their instructional preparation. In reality, questioning skills are rarely developed without intention, and good questions are rarely asked on the fly without purposeful planning. And although any teacher can ask a great question once in a while, the power of strategic questioning in the formative assessment process comes from tightly linking questions to the learning targets and framing them in ways that help students become accountable for contributing to meaningful conversations about important content.

Strategic talking points school leaders can use to address this misconception include the following:

- Strategic questioning is a skill that takes planning and careful teacher observation to develop over time.
- Strategic questions are carefully planned to connect to the specific learning targets in ways that inform student learning.

Misconception #3: Quality, formative discussions are the rule of thumb rather than the exception to the rule in the classroom. Research reveals that teachers routinely overestimate the quality of their classroom discourse. High-quality discussions that advance student learning rarely occur in elementary and secondary classrooms, happening only 4 percent to 8 percent of the time (Dillon, 1984). In other words, more than 90 percent of the time, teachers are not leading the kinds of formative discussions that can raise student achievement and help students learn how to learn.

Strategic talking points school leaders can use to address this misconception include the following:

- High-quality discussions occur infrequently and should be a goal for all teachers.
- Teachers can promote student learning and achievement by focusing their energies on developing formative discussion strategies.

What Is the Motivation Connection?

When teachers frame questions in ways that advance learning, increase student participation, and help students gauge where they are in relation to the learning target, they give students important opportunities to increase self-efficacy, regulate their own learning, and attribute their successes to the learning strategies they use and the amount of effort they put into the learning task. And because strategic questioning involves the use of appropriate wait time, it increases students' confidence in their ability to respond in meaningful ways (Rowe, 2003).

Teachers who plan for and ask strategic questions also increase their own ability to listen to what their students are saying rather than listening for the answers they expect. In this way, they can continue to improve their own questioning skills by varying the kinds of questions they ask, making sure all students feel accountable and confident enough to respond, and helping students learn from each other's thinking. It is difficult to consistently monitor students' learning while responding to students and keeping focused on the learning targets of the lesson. When teachers plan their questions rather than improvise them, they promote classroom discussions that are focused and formative and that actively engage their students in learning how to learn.

What Are Specific Strategies I Can Share with Teachers?

Three strategies that can help teachers to become aware of and improve their use of strategic questioning are (1) taking a questioning snapshot, (2) using appropriate wait time, and (3) following strategic questions with planned thinking extenders.

Taking a Questioning Snapshot

Ask teachers to choose a lesson that will involve whole-class questioning during a discussion. Ask them to pair with a partner teacher who can observe the lesson or to use a recording device to capture the lesson so they can self-assess. Provide them with the sheet titled "Taking a Questioning Snapshot" (Figure 6.2) to aid them in revealing their questioning patterns, assessing their effectiveness, and setting goals for improvement.

Using Strategies That Promote Wait Time

There are three straightforward strategies you can encourage teachers to use that introduce appropriate wait time to their classroom discussions. First, teachers can adopt the *Thinking Time, No Hands Up* strategy. To do this, the teacher

FIGURE 6.2
Taking a Questioning Snapshot

Questioning Pattern	Implications for Student Learning
I talk most of the time without asking a question, or I ask few questions that actually require an answer.	When you monopolize classroom talk with questions that do not require thoughtful responses (e.g., Is everyone with me?), you do not encourage students to think, share opinions, or self-assess.
I ask too many questions, too quickly.	When you employ a quick-fire delivery and bombard your students with questions, their responses tend to be knee-jerk reactions connected to shallow thinking. Asking low-level questions in quick succession does not compel students to think and reason.
I ask too many simple yes/no or agree/disagree questions.	Students have a 50-50 chance of answering correctly without paying attention, and they know it. Simple binary-choice questions do not hold learners accountable for producing, explaining, or justifying a thoughtful response.
I only call on students who raise their hands or volunteer.	Students learn quickly that when they do not raise their hands, the teacher does not hold them responsible for responding. An all-volunteer pattern ensures that many students will mentally disengage from the discussion.
I call on a student by name before I ask my question.	Once students realize they are not required to respond, they "check out." Instead, ask a good strategic question, give all students a chance to think, and then use a random-selection method (e.g., picking names out of a hat) to increase student engagement and accountability.
If a student cannot answer a question immediately, I call on another student to respond to the question.	By not giving students adequate wait time, you deny them the opportunity to plan a thoughtful response, and you send a message that correct responses are quick and short. You make it clear that certain students are incapable of effective responses and encourage perceptions of low self-efficacy.

FIGURE 6.2
Taking a Questioning Snapshot *(cont.)*

Questioning Pattern	Implications for Student Learning
I do not discuss or analyze incorrect or partially correct responses.	When you fail to examine and discuss misconceptions, partial responses, or inaccurate responses, you lose opportunities to clarify important content, increase conceptual change, and provide high-quality formative feedback to help students self-assess.
I ask questions that are off target or that do not promote critical thinking about important concepts and ideas.	Asking questions that are unrelated to the learning target dilutes the discussion and confuses student thinking. Asking low-level, closed questions does little to advance analytical reasoning and the problem-solving skills necessary for academic success.
I am the only one asking questions.	If students are not asking questions—of you and of one another—they do not view learning as a process of getting one's questions answered and are not using the discussion to speculate, reason, form a hypothesis, or seek clarity.

---

explains that she is going to ask a question that will require thinking time in order for students to come up with effective responses. She tells her students that during thinking time, a "no hands up" rule will be in effect. Then the teacher poses a meaty, higher-order question and asks her students to consider it carefully and write down what they are thinking. Then she uses a random-selection method to call on several students to share their prepared responses.

A second strategy is called *Pair Thinking, No Hands Up.* To use this strategy, the teacher assigns, or students choose, a thinking buddy or partner. The teacher asks a good, open, high-level question. The students think with their partners for three to five minutes, making notes about what they considered and the conclusions they reached. Then the teacher uses a random-selection method to call on several thinking pairs to share their jointly created responses.

Finally, teachers can use *Square Thinking, No Hands Up.* To start, the teacher assigns, or students choose, a thinking partner. The teacher asks a strategic question. Students think in pairs for three to five minutes and then join another pair to form a four-student thinking square. The thinking squares have three to five minutes to share their thoughts before the teacher randomly calls on several thinking squares to unpack their thinking and their conclusions for the class.

Following Strategic Questions with Planned Thinking Extenders

Strategic teacher questioning gets students thinking and engages them in formative discussions. The power of the questions is multiplied when teachers plan for and use strategies to extend thinking, deepen the conversation, and keep the discussion moving. More specifically, here are some of the various purposes thinking extenders may have and examples of what a teacher might say in each case:

- Inviting students to elaborate and offer more information
    - Ophelia, please tell us a little more about that.
    - Now that you have heard Rachael's ideas, what are you thinking?
    - Thinking about what Nicholas had to say, it might be useful if we knew more about _____.

- Reinforcing useful ideas, processes, or concepts contained in a response
    - I especially liked Tristan's ideas about ___ because _____.
    - I think Lily used a great strategy for ___ because ___.

- Encouraging further questioning and speculation
    - I wonder what might happen if _____.
    - What Mackenzie said makes me curious about _____.

- Modeling how to summarize
    - Ryan seems to be saying that _____.
    - Nicole, is it fair to say that you conclude that _____?

- Reflecting on the use of a certain strategy or process
    - This time we thought about _____. Maybe the next time we approach something like this we could _____.

Teachers can also use nonverbal cues—eye contact, nodding, raising their eyebrows, smiling—to invite students to enter the discussion, to encourage extended or alternative responses, or to challenge or to express surprise.

How Will I Recognize Strategic Teacher Questioning When I See It?

There are several ways to identify when teachers are using strategic questioning:

- Look for high levels of student engagement in class discussions.
- Listen for responses that are thoughtful and more fully developed.
- Notice teachers' use of specific strategies to ensure appropriate wait time.
- Expect to see teachers using follow-up strategies that extend thinking and keep discussions moving.
- Look for evidence of question design and framing in lesson plans.
- Listen for questions that are directly related to the lesson's learning target.
- Listen for questions that focus student attention on important concepts and processes.
- Listen for questions that encourage students to self-assess.
- Listen for questions that encourage students to comment or elaborate on another student's response.

How Can I Model Strategic Questioning in My Conversations with Teachers About Their Own Professional Learning?

Many school leaders fall into all too common questioning ruts when they lead faculty meetings and teacher professional development days. To make sure professional conversations have the intended outcomes, school leaders should take the time to plan for and frame strategic questions. Like classroom teachers, leaders often overestimate the quality of the discussions that actually occur in a meeting. Strategic questions can make the difference between discourse that is superficial or off topic and lively conversations that are organized, focused, and outcome-driven.

To begin, plan and precisely state the targets for your meeting. You can use the information in Chapter 2 to guide you. Once you have your targets, plan questions that focus like a laser beam on engaging teachers in a critical discussion of the themes and concepts that are essential to your targets. Then frame the questions in clear professional language, keep them open, and draft a few follow-up strategies that you will use to keep the conversation moving in the right direction. Powerful questions not only frame strategic conversations with teachers; they also generate curiosity, surface underlying assumptions, and stimulate thought-provoking generative dialogue. The checklist and illustrative examples in Figure 6.3 can help you plan strategic questions for discussions with individual teachers, small groups, or your entire faculty.

You can make the conversation more equitable and help teachers to be more accountable for sustaining the discussion by coming up with a plan for eliciting responses from all teachers. Trust us, they will thank you. Who has not sat through seemingly endless faculty meetings that were dominated by the same few outspoken people or that rambled along without a clear purpose in sight? By planning for and using strategies that direct teachers to think and prepare their thoughts before the discussion, you are signaling to all who attend that you expect to hear from everyone and you expect responses to be thoughtful and on topic. You can communicate this message even more strongly if you use structured activities or random-selection strategies to invite responses. For example, you can use a pair-share strategy to gain structured input. To get started, put people in pairs, pose a question, have pairs prepare a response, and then ask each pair to share their thoughts, including what they considered as they grappled with the question. During the meeting, change the pairings often to keep the dynamics fresh. You can also use a random-selection process by simply putting names on slips of paper. Pose your question and give people time to prepare a thoughtful response. Then draw names at random to respond. With either strategy, if you run out of time to share responses, you can easily collect everyone's written thoughts. You will be surprised at the difference various questioning and random-selection strategies can make in leading and sustaining a meaningful discussion.

FIGURE 6.3
Leading Discussions with Focus Questions and Conversation Extenders

Action Step	Example/Explanation	Focus Questions	Follow-Up Extenders
1. State the focus of the meeting as a learning target.	• All participants will be able to describe the benefits of formative assessment.	• *What are some observations you've made this week regarding the use of formative assessment in your classroom?*	• *Please share more about that . . .* • *Who can share a similar observation?* • *I imagine some of you can describe a different observation.*
2. Identify the two or three most essential concepts related to your target.	• Formative assessment happens when teachers enter into learning partnerships with their students. • Formative assessment must happen minute by minute and day to day in the classroom.	• *As you think about the ways you are interacting with your students, what new working assumptions seem to be guiding those interactions?* • *What opportunities can you see for us to consistently and intentionally embed formative assessment into the daily heartbeat of our classrooms?*	• *What's taking shape? What are you hearing underneath the variety of opinions being expressed?* • *What's the next level of thinking we need to do to help us become even more consistent and more effective?*
3. Plan one or two questions that will help teachers make important connections or deepen their insights.	• The purpose of strategic questioning is to help generate more questions and out-of-the-box thinking.	• *What did we discuss today that surprised you?* • *What seems to be missing? What points didn't we make or discuss that we should address before we close our discussion?*	• *Tell us more about why you find this so surprising in light of our goals surrounding formative assessment.* • *Why is this so crucial to our progress? What might we risk if we don't address it?*
4. Plan a question that will propel thinking forward and help teachers envision the conversation points for the next meeting.	• You can use strategic questioning to create new boxes from which to think outside!	• *What unique contributions could each of us make to our collective and individual professional growth surrounding formative assessment?*	• *Considering that idea, what support would you need? What support could you give?*

What If?

Strategic teacher questions have the power to advance learning, increase student engagement, and help learners assess where they are in relation to the learning target. *What if you have a teacher or group of teachers who are reluctant to break from traditional teaching structures to engage their students in more classroom discourse?* As you approach this issue, understand that teachers may have many reasons for their reluctance to move from traditional closed questions to questions that encourage all students to participate in an open discussion. Teachers often worry about the consequences of effective questions, which include the increased noise or buzz of engaged discussions; a perceived lack of control; the possibility of misinformation circulating during the discussion; taking time away from content coverage; and the problem of knowing which students are engaged, as active listening is not as overt an activity as answering a direct question. Analyzing the issue from many possible points of view can also help you address teacher concerns.

First, share the common misconceptions about strategic questioning with the teachers. Talk about the ways that effective questions generate student thinking and motivate students to construct high-quality responses. Agree with them that as the classroom becomes a place for lively discussion focused by planned and invigorating teacher questions, they may have to develop new strategies for covering content. Asking effective questions, like formative assessment, is not something you add to what you are already doing. It requires a fundamental reframing of what it means to teach and what we accept as evidence of learning. Assure them that you are not asking them to change everything they do, but rather to use effective teacher questions to transform the classroom into a more vital and valuable environment for them and their students.

You can use many of the strategies in this chapter to help teachers become more effective in asking strategic questions. You can also use feedback from walk-throughs and formal classroom observations to suggest the next steps each teacher can take to stretch a bit without completely leaving the comfort zone. One idea would be to suggest that the teacher plan one or two substantive, open-ended questions to stimulate discussion and then adjust the lesson plan so that the traditional lecture is followed by an open discussion of 10 or 15 minutes, in either group or whole-class format, based on the questions.

Whatever you suggest, the important point is to encourage and expect the teacher to incorporate strategic questioning. Know that teachers will be reluctant for a host of reasons. Listen carefully to those reasons and provide suggestions that are appropriate and supportive.

Reflecting on Strategic Teacher Questioning

The formative assessment process helps students develop inquiry skills that will enable them to continue learning throughout life. As you reflect on strategic teacher questioning as an essential element in the formative assessment process, consider the following questions:

- Do teachers' lesson plans include a list of strategic questions that are closely tied to the learning targets in order to engage students with crucial concepts in meaningful ways? Or do teachers commonly "shoot from the hip," asking random questions that may or may not lead students to a deeper understanding of the important concepts of the lesson?
- Do teachers consistently monitor and refine the quality of the questions they ask and the questioning strategies they employ in order to better help students learn how to learn? Or do they commonly view teacher questions as vehicles for determining which students can recite the correct responses and which students are paying attention?
- Do teachers employ a growing repertoire of techniques to provide appropriate wait time after posing a good, meaty, open-ended question? Or do teachers routinely use rapid-fire techniques with virtually no wait time, thereby promoting short responses from the same small group of students?
- Do you have a plan for sharing research on specific formative assessment strategies with teachers (for example, research on wait time and its effects on student achievement)? How can you be a more effective resource on research-based practices for the teachers you serve?

Summing It Up

The research is painfully clear: In spite of numerous inservice workshops and well-written how-to resources on asking effective questions, in too many cases, teacher questioning and class discussions lack quality and rigor. In most classrooms, teachers are still using low-level, rapid-fire recall questions that require a quick response and minimize student engagement with important content and modes of reasoning.

The formative assessment process gives school leaders a comprehensive and transformational way to help teachers incorporate strategic questions into the heartbeat of their classrooms. The process is comprehensive and transformational because it approaches strategic teacher questions as being integral to helping students learn where they are, where they are headed, and how to take the next best steps in that learning journey.

But in the formative assessment process, teachers are only half of the learning partnership. Helping teachers become strategic questioners takes us only halfway to our goal. Our students must see questioning as a productive way to contribute to classroom dialogue and, most important, as a mind tool for learning. Chapter 7 explores the role of student questioning and the effect it can have on learning and motivation. Together, Chapters 6 and 7 provide crucial insights for enriching classroom talk, developing productive habits of mind, and promoting optimal learning environments in which teachers and students share responsibility for the learning.

7

VALUING CRITICAL THINKING AND INQUIRY:
Engaging Students in Asking Effective Questions

Picture a typical classroom on a typical day during a typical class discussion. Picture the teacher holding a ball of yarn in her hand. As the discussion unfolds, the teacher asks a question and tosses the ball of yarn to the responder, who tosses it back to the questioner. Then the next question is asked. Each time a question-response interaction occurs, the unraveling ball of yarn leaves a trail of the discussion pattern. In this typical classroom, the teacher functions as questioner-in-chief—the talk moves from and back to the teacher, creating a pattern similar to those created by the light rays of the sun (see Figure 7.1). This pattern of classroom talk is all too familiar—teacher question, student response, teacher evaluation, next teacher question. In fact, in many classrooms, the teacher takes up at least two-thirds of the available airtime. And in some classrooms, teachers are the only ones talking, with some teachers actually discouraging discussion, leaving students "talk-deprived" (Alvermann et al., 1996).

Now picture a classroom where the formative assessment process is alive and well. Students in this classroom see their questions as mind tools for the job of learning because their teacher encourages their questions as indicators of powerful thinking. Questions are valued in this classroom, and questions are asked *by* and *of* all learners. The pattern of talk in this classroom bears little resemblance to a single-source, ray-of-light pattern signaling that the teacher controls the learning. In fact, in this classroom there is no set talk pattern. But if we had to describe it,

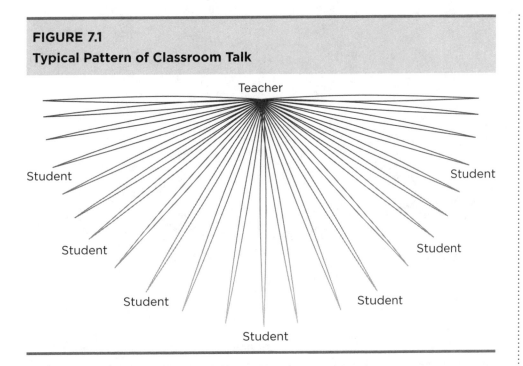

FIGURE 7.1
Typical Pattern of Classroom Talk

we would say it most closely resembles a free-form web (see Figure 7.2). And on any given day, the exact interactions the web depicts depend on the questions that the learners generate in pursuit of the learning target.

In classrooms where the formative assessment process is alive and well, the teacher is not the only skilled questioner. In fact, the teacher strives for democratic discourse that is vibrant and meaningful and that encourages students to think deeply and ask powerful questions.

What Does It Mean to Engage Students in Asking Effective Questions?

Students who ask effective questions recognize, value, and employ questioning as a productive mind tool to increase their understanding of important content and concepts. Learning to ask effective questions is central to the formative assessment process. Teachers cannot teach (and students cannot learn) everything there is to know. That is why engaging students in asking effective questions and teaching them strategies for doing so are critical, finally enabling us to give more than

FIGURE 7.2
Inquiry Discussion Web

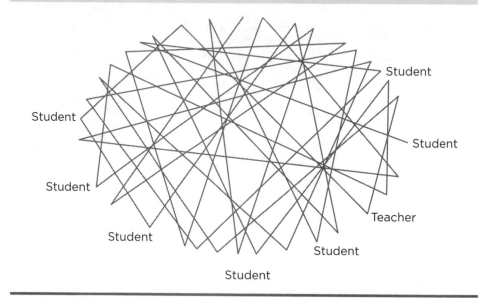

casual lip service to the concept of developing lifelong learners. When students use self-questioning as they read and study independently, they deepen their understanding. And when learners are regularly engaged in collaborative inquiry discussions that they truly care about—discussions that are relevant and engaging and involve content central to the learning target—they are full of questions.

Walk into any kindergarten on any day and you will witness children asking thousands of questions—lines of inquiry that involve their teacher, their peers, and any visitor. Young children are full of questions and not shy about making sure they get their questions answered. Quite a different experience occurs if you observe a typical high school classroom and listen for the student questions. If you hear one, it is likely to be about the mechanics of an assignment or the steps in a task or simply "Will this be on the test?"

What happens to our students as they make their way from their first day of school to their high school graduation? Why do they lose their urgency for asking questions? Surely something that we do in schools contributes to this all too common phenomenon. What is it that dampens their curiosity and encourages them *not* to question? What happens to students that "breaks them to saddle"—tames their natural instincts to explore, wonder, and investigate—to create passive receivers of knowledge? How can we reignite their curiosity and reintroduce them to the power of effective questions? What if we not only taught content but also valued and developed student learning based on inquiry? If we did, we would approach our students as engaged and empowered questioners, helping them develop and practice strategies for seeking clarity and using their curiosity about a topic to deepen their understanding.

Learning to use effective questions as powerful learning tools requires students to develop the three sides of the effective questioner: knowledge, skill, and will, or disposition (see Figure 7.3). Simply put, students must be ready, willing, and able to ask effective questions in order to succeed. Developing only one area will not do.

We can illustrate the importance of the bond among the three sides of the effective questioner by using a simple example that examines the task of flossing teeth. First, ask yourself: *Do I know what dental floss is, and can I describe how to use it?* If you answered yes, then you have sound flossing knowledge—you are *ready* to floss. Next, ask yourself: *Have I ever tried to floss my teeth or practiced*

FIGURE 7.3
Triad Model of an Engaged and Effective Student Questioner

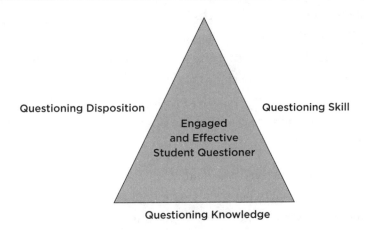

flossing my teeth in a way that could be described as effective flossing? If you answered yes, then you have the skill to floss—you are *able* to floss your teeth. Now the final question: *Do I floss my teeth after each meal or snack?* If you are typical when it comes to flossing, you responded to the last question by admitting that you do not. In other words, you are *ready* to floss and you are certainly *able* to floss, but you are not *willing* to floss—you are not disposed to flossing regularly. You do not have the disposition of an effective flosser.

When we talk about engaging students in asking effective questions, we must also talk about simultaneously developing the three sides of the effective student questioner. Students learn through inquiry because they have questioning knowledge; they are capable of asking questions in pursuit of their own learning and understanding; and, most important, they are disposed to asking effective questions—of themselves, their teachers, and their peers—as part of the day-to-day, minute-by-minute work they do in the classroom.

How Does Engaging Students in Asking Effective Questions Affect Student Learning and Achievement?

We learn by asking questions. We learn better by asking better questions. We learn more by having opportunities to ask more questions (Morgan & Saxton, 1991). Teaching students to develop their own questioning skills and encouraging them to ask effective questions as a regular part of classroom talk help them become increasingly active in their own learning. Armed with self-assessment skills and using information from feedback that feeds forward, learners are more in tune with what and how much they know and understand about a topic. And because they are deeply engaged, students recognize how clearly they understand and what more they need to learn in order to apply their new understandings to unique and novel situations. As students develop the knowledge, skills, and dispositions of effective questioners, they also do the following (Clarke, 2005; Hale & City, 2006; Spiegel, 2005):

- Develop independence and autonomy.
- Construct deeper and richer meaning for important content and concepts.
- Take more responsibility for their own learning.
- Learn and practice discipline-specific ways of thinking.

- Discover how to persist during a challenge by seeking accuracy and clarity.
- Explain and express themselves more easily.
- Think deeply about what they are trying to achieve and master.
- Seek explanations and alternatives more frequently.
- Use self-assessment to monitor and evaluate their own understanding.

Finally, even though students learn by asking questions, without developing the ability to do that in effective and confident ways, they will continue to use what David Perkins (1995) calls "everyday thinking." If we leave students to their own devices, they seldom become skilled thinkers. They have powerful minds but lack the means to harness their thinking in ways that enable them to reason deeply with greater effectiveness and rise above everyday thinking. Everyday thinking is like walking. It is something we can all do without conscious thought and with little need to increase our skill. But skilled thinking—the kind of thinking that students use when they generate effective questions—is like running the 100-yard dash. Skilled thinking requires technique, intentional effort, practice, self-regulation, and the use of self-assessment, goal setting, and increasingly sophisticated thinking strategies.

Skilled thinking and effective questioning are two sides of the same coin. In fact, there is a strong relationship between effective questioning, skilled thinking, and student achievement (Bransford, Brown, & Cocking, 2000; Hunkins, 1995). Skilled thinkers achieve more because they think about their own thinking and constantly seek to improve it. It takes this kind of skilled, metacognitive thinking for students to generate effective questions.

What Are Some Common Misconceptions That Teachers Might Hold About Teaching Students to Ask Powerful Questions?

The notable lack of student questioning as a vital and central feature of how learning happens in the classroom can be traced to common misconceptions teachers hold about student questioning.

Misconception #1: If students are encouraged to ask questions, they will take the conversation off topic, use up precious learning time, and

make it impossible to cover the content on schedule. Student questions hold contradictory meanings for teachers as conflicting forces come into play in a political landscape that holds teachers increasingly accountable to mounting curricular pressures. Although teachers say they value thoughtful questions about lesson content and concepts, they often view questions as interruptions to the normal flow of the classroom and a threat to their ability to control content coverage and lesson pacing.

Strategic talking points school leaders can use to address this misconception include the following:

- Even though student questions are a way to put students in the driver's seat, the teacher is still there to steer the conversation, apply the brakes, and accelerate the pace.
- The teacher is turning over some of the responsibility for learning, not relinquishing total control over the content and direction of classroom conversations.

Misconception #2: Students do not know enough about the content to ask good questions. Although teachers might enthusiastically endorse the idea that inquiry should grow and flourish in classrooms where student questions are encouraged and respected, research suggests that teacher beliefs about the nature of student questioning often prevent inquiry from actually taking root (e.g., Rop, 2002).

Strategic talking points school leaders can use to address this misconception include the following:

- The kinds of conversations that are fertile ground for student questions take place after students have spent some time with the topic and concepts.
- Students prepare their questions as a normal part of learning about the content, assessing their knowledge, receiving good feedback, and setting and getting their own learning goals.

Misconception #3: The same people will ask all the questions and monopolize the conversation. In classrooms where inquiry is neither promoted nor encouraged, it is common for the same few students to answer all the teacher's questions. Teachers might conclude, therefore, that these same students will ask all the questions in a classroom where student questioning *is* encouraged. Actually, the reverse is true. Once all students are taught how to frame and ask effective questions, a culture of inquiry begins to develop where all students are active participants in quality conversations focused on the learning targets.

Strategic talking points school leaders can use to address this misconception include the following:

- Teaching students the skills of good questioning will actually increase student participation.
- Part of teaching students to ask effective questions involves helping them learn to listen respectfully and critically to each other in ways that maximize student participation.

Teacher misconceptions are inflamed by the tension teachers feel about handing over control of what happens in their classrooms. They are skeptical about putting students in the driver's seat because they see their students as lacking the knowledge, skill, and will to learn through effective questioning. Addressing these misconceptions head-on will help teachers come to grips with the crucial need to teach and encourage students to ask powerful questions as an important part of the formative assessment process.

What Is the Motivation Connection?

The level of motivation students bring to a topic will be transformed, for better or for worse, by what happens every day in the classroom. Even with topics that might appear to be naturally stimulating, students' excitement and curiosity can be dampened if teachers create learning situations that expect the students to passively learn the content in the way it is handed to them.

Students have two primary incentives to ask academic questions: to get help when they are stuck or confused, or to get more information when they are curious. Either way, asking a question takes high levels of self-efficacy—students must believe in their own questioning competence (Newman & Goldin, 1990).

When students engage in the cognitive work required to frame a question about important content and concepts, they are deeply engaged in meaning making. To ask an effective question, students must think critically, connect new information to what they already know about a topic, and experience learning as understanding. Framing and asking a powerful question requires students to make connections between the content and their personal interests and experiences, thereby deepening relevance and increasing intrinsic motivation to learn (Perkins, 1992; Wells, 2001).

In fact, when students are actively involved in constructing and posing effective questions, they embody motivation to learn. They demonstrate a genuine desire to know more than they already know and to move beyond the information given to think about content in new and novel ways (Barell, 2003). As students begin to see themselves as effective questioners who can ask questions to deepen their understanding and enhance their own thinking, they become more aware of and responsible for their own knowledge and thoughts. In other words, engaging students in generating effective questions helps them to perceive themselves as autonomous and independent learners, producers of knowledge, and generators of important lines of inquiry. Developing as effective questioners gives students increased confidence that they can work through difficulties themselves. They learn to attribute their successes and their failures to factors that they can control and change.

What Are Specific Strategies I Can Share with Teachers?

As we noted earlier, there are three sides of the effective student questioner that the formative assessment process helps to develop. What follows are strategies that have particular strength in developing these three areas. Although we tried to organize the strategies based on their strongest influence on the effective questioner, many of the strategies we suggest help students develop more than one side of their questioning effectiveness and often help develop the three sides simultaneously.

Strategies for Developing Knowledge About Asking Questions

It is important for students to understand that learning is a process that involves getting questions answered. But asking effective questions isn't easy or natural for most students. Many students have had little practice with asking questions and are not sure about the mechanics of framing a question or where effective questions come from. The two strategies we suggest here help students understand that questions arise naturally when they approach new content, think about concepts, try new processes or procedures, or learn more about concepts and ideas that are familiar to them.

The *Question Starters* strategy helps students build and expand their questioning repertoire by exposing them to and helping them practice using the kinds of beginning phrases that often start meaty, effective questions. To use this strategy, teachers distribute question starters on note cards, strips of paper, fun shapes, or simply a handout. Students can use the question starters to prepare questions about a topic before or during a class discussion. Figure 7.4 provides examples for several different categories of questions.

An updated *SQ3R (Scan-Question-Read-Relate-Reflect)* strategy, based on the original work of Francis P. Robinson (1941), provides both modeling and guided practice in framing strong questions that are related to the content students study and the books they read to gain information about that content. SQ3R walks students through the process of moving from a textbook passage to forming questions that, if answered, will help them understand the content and the crucial concepts at a much deeper level. Teachers can supply the SQ3R guide (Figure 7.5) for students to use as they read in preparation for a class discussion or a collaborative learning activity. Using the SQ3R strategy helps students become effective questioners and strong metacognitive learners who do the following:

- Notice when they lose focus.
- Stop and go back to clarify thinking.
- Reread through the lens of an effective question to enhance understanding.
- Identify and articulate what's confusing about a concept.
- Actively use self-questioning strategies to restore comprehension.

Strategies for Developing Effective Questioning Skills

The ability to frame a good question comes with practice. The more questions we frame, the better we become at framing questions. The same goes for becoming skillful at asking the questions that we have prepared. Most students have little skill as questioners because they are rarely expected to raise questions. The primary strategy, then, is for teachers to consistently engage students in collaborative

FIGURE 7.4
Question Starters by Category

Question Category	Question Starters
Observation and Recall	• What did you notice about _____? • What do you remember about _____? • How did ____? • What did you find out about _____?
Relationships and Organizing	• How are ____ and ____ similar/different? • What belongs together? Why do you think so? • What happened to cause _____? • What events led up to _____? • How does ____ apply to everyday life?
Summarizing and Drawing Conclusions	• What conclusions can I draw about ____? • What is another way we could say/explain/express that? • What is the best ____, and why?
Predicting, Inferring, and Anticipating	• What feeling do you think made ____ act that way? • Judging from the title/picture, what do you think is about to happen? • If we changed ____, what do you think would/would not happen? Why?

learning activities that require students to ask questions and scaffold them as they practice questioning in a safe and supportive environment. The following strategies will be useful to teachers as they help their students develop their skills as effective, collaborative questioners.

The *Questioning Quads* strategy allows learners to practice generating questions and asking questions as they work together to construct meaning. The questioning structure involves students in making predictions and discussing what they read to foster active engagement and critical thinking. And because the students are directing the discussion, the teacher is free to observe, scaffold, and reinforce the questioning strategies that the students use.

To begin, put learners into groups of four. Ask the students to read silently to an appropriate place in the text chosen beforehand by the teacher. When the students

FIGURE 7.5
Steps of the SQ3R Prediscussion Strategy

Steps	What to Do
Scan	**Before you read . . .** • Scan the entire passage, chapter, or assigned reading in detail. • Consider the title, headings, pictures, graphs, and questions included at the end of the reading. What does it all add up to tell you? • What do you think you are supposed to learn from the reading?
Question	**Before you read . . .** • List three important points about the content of this passage that you discovered during your scan. • Write a question about each important point that you will try to answer as you read. • Jot down information that helps to answer your three questions as you read.
R1—Read	**After you read . . .** • Ask yourself, *What did I already know about this topic that was not in the reading?* • Write two questions that will help you learn more about what you already knew.
R2—Relate	**As you reread . . .** • Jot down information that helps to answer your questions about the important points and relates to what you already knew.
R3—Reflect	**After rereading . . .** • Ask yourself, *What don't I still understand? What don't I agree with, and why?* • Write five questions that you will bring to the class discussion to deepen your own learning and the learning of your classmates.

finish reading, they begin the questioning quad using question strips like the ones suggested in Figure 7.6. Student 1 is the *questioner*. He chooses a questioning strip at random and uses the phrase to frame a question that either asks about what the group read or can be used to predict what might, will, or can happen next. Student 2 is the *paraphraser*. She puts the question into her own words. Student 3 is the *responder*. This student answers the question that Student 1 asked and Student 2 rephrased. Finally, Student 4 gives feedback by describing what the group learned

---

FIGURE 7.6
Questioning Quad Strips

• I wonder if . . .	• How did . . .
• I wonder when . . .	• What is your opinion . . .
• Why do you think . . .	• Why is the picture . . .
• I wonder who . . .	• Can you take a guess . . .
• I wonder how . . .	• What happened when . . .
• What would happen if . . .	• Who found . . .
• What if . . .	• Who tried to . . .
• Why did the author . . .	• When was . . .
• Do you understand why . . .	• Can you remember why . . .
• How were . . .	• When did you begin to think . . .
• How did . . .	• Why would it be necessary to . . .
• How many other ways . . .	• Why was it important that . . .
• When did you realize . . .	• How do you explain . . .
• What happened before . . .	• What was unique about . . .
• When will . . .	• What puzzled you about . . .

---

by asking and responding to the question. Once the quad is complete, the students rotate roles and tackle a new passage.

The *My Contribution Roles and Goals* strategy sets a learning target for each student that involves asking good questions, responding politely to the questions that others ask, and listening respectfully when others are contributing to the discussion. Give each student a "contribution meter" for self-assessment before, during, and after a class or group discussion. Although the example we share in Figure 7.7 is appropriate for elementary and middle school students, the same points apply to high school discussions and can be shared as a simple checklist.

After the students complete the self-assessment of their discussion roles, encourage them to set goals for what they intend to do better, more of, or differently in the next discussion. Teachers can also use the completed forms to lead a class discussion on the use of effective questioning skills.

FIGURE 7.7
Contribution Meter

Discussion Skills	My Contribution Level		
	I am beginning	I am better at	I am very good at
• I listen respectfully to what others say.	❏	❏	❏
• I do not interrupt—it is important to let others finish what they want to say.	❏	❏	❏
• If I have a different point of view, I express it politely (*I agree because . . .*, or *I disagree because . . .*, or *I was thinking about that another way . . .*).	❏	❏	❏
• If someone disagrees with me, I listen and try to think it through from their point of view.	❏	❏	❏
• I make sure not to ask all the questions or try to answer all the questions that are asked. The more people who are part of the discussion, the more we will all learn.	❏	❏	❏
• I use good eye contact—when someone asks a question, I look at them so they know I am interested in what they are saying and appreciate their contribution.	❏	❏	❏
• I ask a "piggy-back" question when someone's question or response makes me want to learn more. (*Can you talk more about . . . ?*)	❏	❏	❏
• I answer questions with important facts and information that I learned by reading and studying or through an important experience.	❏	❏	❏
• I give my opinion about issues when it is appropriate and back up my opinions with facts and examples.	❏	❏	❏
• I prepare for the discussion by preparing my questions beforehand and then use the discussion to help me get my questions answered.	❏	❏	❏
My Goals for Improving My Contribution			

Strategies for Developing the Disposition to Learn Through Effective Questioning

It may sound simple at first, but for students to be willing to ask their questions, they must feel welcome and safe. The most important strategy teachers can use to help students develop a disposition to ask questions is to create an open and supportive classroom environment where student questioning is valued and encouraged.

The Questioning Climate Checklist (Figure 7.8) is a useful tool for teachers. It will help them assess what they do to encourage *all* students to ask questions and uncover what they might be doing to deter the free exchange of ideas in their classroom. School leaders can use the same list of questions to focus teacher observations or to guide discussions about the importance of encouraging active student questioning as a viable and vital part of the learning process.

How Will I Recognize Effective Student Questioning When I See It?

As we mentioned previously, a good way to identify effective student questioning is to become familiar with the characteristics of classroom climates that foster student questioning. Using the Questioning Climate Checklist is a good way to do that.

But climate is only part of the equation. You can also look and listen for the following:

- Do student questions focus on the mechanics of an assignment or lesson, or do they go to the heart of important concepts or content?
- Do students seem interested and engaged?
- Do students ask their questions in ways that show confidence and competence?
- Do teachers have dedicated time (in lesson plans or on schedules) to focus on question development and guidance?
- Do you see signs of structure and scaffolded inquiry—formats that shape and encourage effective questioning?

Students and teachers cannot fake the knowledge, skill, or will to learn together by asking and responding to powerful questions. If the process seems awkward

FIGURE 7.8
Questioning Climate Checklist

Threat Level
• Do my students feel safe and free to ask the questions they want to ask?
• Do my students hear me say things that invite them to ask questions or that praise them for their contributions?

Practice Level
• Do I provide my students a chance to practice questioning and responding to questions in pairs or small groups?
• Do I give my students time to prepare their questions before a discussion?

Modeling Level
• Do I model good questioning skills, knowledge, and dispositions for my students?
• Do I respond to student questions with genuine interest and respect?

Resource Level
• Do I provide questioning resources that help my students use appropriate vocabulary or phrases to frame their questions?
• Do I provide my students with self-questioning structures that help them learn to use questioning as an integral part of self-assessment?

Feedback Level
• Do I regularly give my students informative feedback on their development as effective questioners?
• Do I provide specific suggestions and strategies to help my students take the just-right next step in their journey to become effective questioners?

Opportunity Level
• Do I monopolize the airtime by doing most of the talking or asking most of the questions?
• Do I have specific strategies for providing equal opportunities for all students to ask and respond to questions?

Wait-Time Level
• Do I provide time for my students to think before inviting a response?
• Do I implement specific strategies for using and encouraging appropriate wait time?

Honesty Level
• When I am unsure of an answer, do I admit to my students that I honestly do not know?
• Do I turn questions I cannot answer into teachable moments that help my students learn how to get their questions answered?

or unnatural, then it probably isn't happening with frequency, feedback, or encouragement.

How Can I Model the Importance of Effective Student Questioning in Conversations with Teachers About Their Own Professional Learning?

We spend far too much time admiring answers in our classrooms when there are many more reasons to admire questions. And, if truth be told, we are guilty of not placing enough value on student questions as an indicator of—a way to assess—significant learning. Why is the thoughtful student question so rare in our classrooms and in our schools?

As we noted earlier, young children come to school with an urgency for learning and a disposition to gain knowledge by getting their questions answered. What changes them? Sadly, the answer is that we educators do; in our schools and our classrooms we constantly send the message that answers are the coin of the realm. And to prove how much we prize the correct answer to each question, we add up the number of correct answers and write the total at the top of their exams to signify the degree of their learning.

Our actions speak volumes. We evaluate what we value. In fact, the process of evaluating literally stands for "placing value" on something. It stands to reason, then, that you can significantly influence what is valued in your school by sending a clear message that optimal learning environments place value on student questions. When talking with teachers, make sure to clearly communicate the value—significance, worth, or quality—that you see and expect in student questions. Ask teachers to share the best questions that students asked that day.

Use conversations with teachers to heighten the value they place on student questions by placing value on them yourself. Talk about the effective student questions you heard or the conversations you observed resulting from those questions. Applaud the planning and great teaching that foster effective student questioning—because it doesn't happen unless the climate is right.

And create a school climate where great questions are part of the culture. Give teachers time to think and frame questions before a meeting or a private conversation. Listen to them politely and let them ask all the questions they want to ask. Treat their questions with respect, and then expect them to extend the same courtesy and encouragement to the students in their care.

Here are some conversation starters you can use in discussions with teachers about the importance of effective student questioning:

- *I know you have been working on integrating formative assessment into the very fabric of your classroom. Think with me for a minute about the kinds of questions your students are asking and about the evidence you are gathering about their ability and willingness to learn through effective questioning.*

- *Walk me through your most recent class discussion. As we think about the kinds of interactions that occurred—who asked the questions and who contributed to the discussion—let's talk about the strategies you are using to help your students develop questioning dispositions and increase their confidence as strategic questioners.*

- *Using what we discussed, let's talk about the opportunities you see for planning and adjusting your instruction in ways that will increase the probability that your students will grow and flourish as effective questioners.*

- *Now that you have specific strategies in mind, let's think a minute about the challenges that might be preventing your students from fully realizing the power of being effective questioners and the kinds of supports we can create to help them meet those challenges head-on.*

What If?

Formative assessment is a process, and, as with any important change, making it part of the minute-by-minute heartbeat of the classroom will take effort over time. That means it is safe to bet that teachers will be at different places along a continuum of implementation, not just in terms of the degree that formative assessment becomes part of the fiber of the classroom but also in terms of the degree that all students are benefitting. *What if you observe a teacher who is not effectively involving students who are English language learners (ELLs) in a class discussion?*

Facilitating equitable class discussions in a multicultural classroom can be daunting for teachers, and contributing to these discussions can raise a myriad of insecurities for linguistically and culturally diverse students. Because formative assessment focuses on helping students learn how to learn, the ideas expressed in this chapter to facilitate student questioning and discourse work very well to encourage more active participation for English learners.

Ask the teacher to think with you about the goals the teacher has for ELLs. Remind the teacher that tying the discussion tightly to the learning targets creates the kind of topically focused discussions that benefit English learners and expose them to important concepts and information. Suggest using the Questioning Quads strategy described in this chapter. This strategy allows students who are learning English to share and rehearse their questions about key concepts with a supportive group of peers to increase learning and to gain skill in asking effective questions. This will help students who are learning English develop motivation to contribute to a whole-class discussion.

Reflecting on Engaging Students in Asking Effective Questions

Memorizing facts and information is not the most important skill in today's world. Facts change; information is readily available. In the 21st century and beyond, learners need an understanding of how to get and make sense of information, concepts, and data. Through the process of inquiry, students learn to construct much of their understanding of the natural and human-designed worlds. Sadly, our students are rarely asked to discover compelling questions, nor do we teach them why they should ask such questions in the first place. As you reflect on engaging students in asking effective questions as an essential element in the formative assessment process, consider the following questions:

- Do teachers provide students with opportunities to learn how to ask great questions and the time to practice those skills during engaging classroom conversations about learning? Or are most classes run in a traditional teacher-directed format in which questions come only from the teacher and great discussions are the exception to the rule?
- Do teachers clearly communicate to their students that they value their questions, respect them as learning partners, and appreciate their efforts to contribute to the teaching-learning process? Or do teachers react

to student questions in ways that say they view student questions as interruptions to the teacher's control over the pacing and direction of the lesson?

- Do teachers build a growing repertoire of strategies for teaching students how to ask effective questions? Do teachers coach students on how to respond and listen respectfully to the questions posed by their peers? Do teachers work consistently to create classroom climates that are open and supportive? Or do teachers expect students to be able to develop questioning knowledge, skills, and dispositions on their own?
- Do you regularly comment on the questioning practices that you observe in your walk-throughs in ways that encourage teachers to plan for and teach students how to become effective questioners?

Summing It Up

It is fitting that the final element of the formative assessment process reminds us to value student questions and the important role they play in assessment *for* learning. Active student questioning takes us full circle. We began with the three guiding questions of the formative assessment process: *Where am I? Where am I going? What strategy or strategies can help me get to where I need to go?* And, it is hoped, we now see those questions with new eyes. If teachers are the only ones who are asking effective questions, then our classrooms are lacking a key ingredient to increasing student achievement—developing students who are competent, confident, and self-regulated learners.

Just as formative assessment can forge powerful learning partnerships in the classroom, it can promote learning partnerships and a culture of collaborative inquiry throughout a school. In the final chapter, we offer practical suggestions and commonsense encouragement for unleashing the power of formative assessment schoolwide.

8

CREATING A CULTURE OF INTENTIONAL LEARNING:
Taking Formative Assessment Schoolwide

We began our discussion of the formative assessment process by comparing it to a windmill. We likened the elements of the process to the blades of a windmill. This apt and vivid metaphor is worth revisiting here. When it comes to effectiveness, the blades of a windmill are the most significant factor. With only one blade, you have nothing. If blades are missing, uneven, or broken, a windmill loses both its effectiveness and its efficiency. A windmill needs all of its blades operating with constancy and dependability and whirring in harmony in order to successfully harness moving air to produce energy.

As school leaders consider the significant effects that the formative assessment process can have on their schools, they must remind themselves that like the blades of a windmill, all the elements must work in unison. Although an element such as effective feedback can certainly have a positive influence, feedback alone is not the formative assessment process. Formative assessment is both driven by and dependent upon the functional bond of the six elements. Without recognizing and understanding learning targets and the criteria for success, teachers and students cannot set goals, ask effective questions, profit from feedback, or have formative discussions. If students are not taught to self-assess or to set goals, then the best feedback in the world cannot propel them forward. And without knowing how to ask effective questions to advance their own learning goals, students cannot become lifelong learners. Like an effective windmill, the formative assessment process derives its power from the fusion of its elements as they work together at the highest levels of quality and precision.

Taking formative assessment schoolwide means that a school leader must steward a process of complex change throughout the school, guiding and supporting the day-to-day and minute-by-minute work of the classroom. To be clear, formative assessment requires more than simply implementing a strategy or two, or implementing only some of the elements, or merely experimenting with all of the elements on a surface level.

Implementing the formative assessment process across a school involves changing the beliefs that teachers hold about how students learn and reframing the role teachers play in supporting that learning. And taking formative assessment schoolwide means replacing vague notions of the administrator as instructional leader with the powerful symbol of a school leader as the leading learner in an intentional learning community. If school leaders are serious about infusing the formative assessment process into the fabric of their schools, they must demonstrate the value they place on learning and consistently support classroom practices that help students learn how to harness the workings of their own minds to become competent and confident learners.

Why Is It Important to Take the Formative Assessment Process Schoolwide?

Chapters 1 through 7 discussed formative assessment in individual classrooms. Taking formative assessment schoolwide is important for both teachers and students. Teachers will feel less isolated and more supported in their formative assessment efforts if they are not going it alone. And students will experience consistency if formative assessment is common practice among the teachers in their school.

The consequences are particularly important for student motivation. If in one class students experience practices that help them see their learning targets clearly and in another class they feel like lessons are "what the teacher decided to do today," they will have uneven opportunities to develop self-regulation skills. If in one class students experience practices that help them understand that it's *their* decisions about what is important to do and about what and how to study that will further their learning, and in another class they feel they are being told what to do, they will at best receive mixed messages and at worst become confused and less motivated.

Most of the studies on which Black and Wiliam's (1998) well-known conclusions about the benefits of formative assessment are based were research projects in which the concepts under study were ways of getting information to *students*. Definitions of schoolwide implementation of formative assessment that are only about getting information to *teachers* for them to use in adjusting instruction (as, for example, in some benchmark or interim assessment programs) stop short of being genuine formative assessment in the sense we have used the term in this book. More important, professional development or other efforts at schoolwide implementation of formative assessment that focus only on teacher use of information for adjusting instruction are not the sort of efforts that the research base for formative assessment says should be effective.

What Does the Research Say About Taking Formative Assessment Schoolwide?

Schoolwide changes in teacher practices require planning, coordination, and nurturing. Popham (2008) recommends teacher professional development and professional learning communities as two strategies for honing individual teachers' formative assessment skills and for schoolwide implementation of formative assessment.

A recent research project confirmed that sustained professional development will be needed for the kinds of changes in practice suggested for formative assessment. Shavelson and his colleagues (2008) theorize that if Black and Wiliam's (1998) findings were heading in the right direction, then embedding formal formative assessments in a nationally recognized science curriculum should lead to improved teaching and increased student learning. Assessment developers at Stanford University worked with curriculum developers at the University of Hawaii to develop formal formative assessments for a unit on buoyancy from the *Foundational Approaches in Science Teaching* (FAST) curriculum. Constructed-response tasks that called for students to interpret graphs and predict, observe, and explain aspects of floating and sinking were designed and embedded in the FAST unit at "joints," or conceptual hinge points, in the lessons' sequence. They called these formative assessments "reflective lessons."

These assessments differed a bit from the formative assessment practices we have been discussing in this book, in both an intentional and an unintentional way. The developers intended that the FAST "reflective lessons" would be more formal than many of the informal observational and conversational techniques we have discussed. They were, after all, predesigning them and embedding them in a prepared curriculum. (We quickly add that "informal" does not mean "unplanned." We hope our chapters have shown that questions for students and in-class strategies need to be planned as a regular part of instruction.)

The developers, however, did not intend the second difference between what happened and what we have been describing as formative assessment in this book. The intention was that the reflective lessons would provide useful information for teachers *and students* about students' understanding of floating and sinking. Teachers received professional development about how to do that. All six teachers in the formative assessment group (there was also a control group of teachers who used the curriculum materials without the formative assessments) in the study thought they were using the curriculum materials, including the formative reflective lessons, as they had been asked to do. And yet the embedded formative assessments did not have an effect, on average, on student motivation, achievement, or conceptual change (Yin et al., 2008).

The lessons of the teachers in the formative assessment group were videotaped, which led to a host of findings (Furtak et al., 2008). We discuss only a few of the findings here, those that speak to the difficulties of implementing formative assessment practices across classrooms, even with some training.

Teachers were asked to hold class discussions during the reflective lessons (the study's formative assessments). Discussions, however, took only about 27 percent of reflective lesson time. Probably more important, discussions were not always held right after the predict-observe-explain or short-answer tasks, the formal formative assessments that had been designed for the study. This was a problem, because this is the point at which the student use of formative assessment information would be expected to happen. Students did not get a chance to process the information from their formative assessment performance.

Other student-centered parts of the formative assessment process became easily derailed, too. Teachers did use a variety of strategies for collecting student ideas and concepts. They did, then, display student ideas, as the curriculum guide asked them to do (for example, by using stickies or a whiteboard or an overhead projector). But only some of the teachers spent any time clustering the ideas, looking for patterns, or otherwise helping the students make sense of the ideas—and then for only a tiny portion of the time. Most of the time teachers did not ask follow-up or "why" questions to ask students to express their reasoning. Most of the time students did not back up their scientific claims with evidence from their classroom work. Finally, most (83 percent) of the time students were talking, they were addressing the teacher rather than other students (Furtak et al., 2008).

If these teachers found it difficult to understand and implement student-centered formative assessment practices, many others probably will, too. In fact, the notion that when it comes to significant learning it matters more what the student does than what the teacher does is a conceptual change that is difficult for most teachers to make at first. So when we recommend taking formative assessment schoolwide, we realize we are talking about a complex change in culture—a change that will require effort over time.

What Should School Leaders Keep in Mind to Increase the Likelihood of Taking Formative Assessment Schoolwide?

School leaders should carefully consider particular characteristics of the formative assessment process as they work daily to change the culture of their school. The bottom line is that formative assessment is a learning process. It is not a prepackaged program with teachers manuals, lesson plans, worksheets, and other materials. It is not something that teachers must *enact* but, rather, something they must *embrace*. Although embracing significant conceptual change about what it means to teach and what we should count as evidence of learning is difficult, it is much more lasting than asking teachers to adopt the next educational trend or buzzword. For too long teachers have taken a "this too shall pass" attitude toward fundamentally changing what they do in their classrooms. They have lived through many waves of reform and seen them fall out of fashion almost as quickly as they arrive.

The formative assessment process is not a new initiative or mandated reform in education. It goes to the heart of what we do in schools and in classrooms when we mount a serious effort to maximize student achievement and motivation to learn. Taking formative assessment schoolwide, therefore, is both essential and challenging. To meet the challenge head-on, it helps to keep the following points in mind.

First, each school is unique. The way change rolls out in one school is not the way it will roll out in another school. Know that going in. Your school, your teachers, your climate, your history—all of these will both determine and inform what it will take to change the culture of your school from teacher-led instruction to a partnership of intentional inquiry. Repurpose the guiding questions of the formative assessment process: *Where is my school now? Where do we want to go? What strategy or strategies will help us get to where we need to go?* Changing what you value in your school depends on where you are now and not on where other schools are. Complex change means capitalizing on your distinctive strengths and addressing your particular areas of need.

A mutual friend tells a cautionary tale about leading change by drawing a comparison to competing in a swim meet. As a father of three competitive swimmers, he explains that seasoned parents can tell when a swimmer compromises her chances of winning. Each swimmer must learn to stay focused on swimming her own race and not give in to the temptation of comparing her progress with the progress of the other swimmers. If a swimmer uses her time to glance at the other competitors during the race, a gasp will rise from the crowd: "Oh no, she looked!" Swimmers lose valuable energy and momentum when they break form to look beside them or behind them.

Your school is unique. Use the mind tip of champion swimmers: *Swim your best by staying focused on swimming your best in your own lane.*

The second point to remember is encapsulated in the saying "You eat an elephant one bite at a time." Taking formative assessment schoolwide may seem overwhelming at first. The process takes time to learn and implement with fidelity and quality. Formative assessment is a complex change, and complex changes do not happen overnight. Change requires trust, and change requires risk. Change takes consistency, understanding, and compassion. Each day is another opportunity to learn more, do better, and collect evidence of success.

Remember that formative assessment is a complex process. It is not a strategy or a technique, and doing it well means implementing the process elements together, with consistency and quality. To do this, teachers learn new ways to think by *unlearning* what they believed to be true about how students learn and how quality teaching supports that learning. You cannot implement the formative assessment process in a day, but you can begin each day with the intention to keep moving forward. Lasting change takes time and commitment. You must be in this for the long haul.

Third, the research is clear: formative assessment increases student achievement. So just do it! Asking teachers to buy in is not the way to go. If just a few teachers in the building put formative assessment into practice, then what about the students in the classrooms of teachers who do not? Should they achieve less? Would we ask medical professionals to choose whether or not they want to share lifesaving practices with their patients? The proposition sounds ridiculous because it is ridiculous. Expect and demand full participation from the outset and stick with it. This book can help you suggest, support, and encourage as your school moves forward with this important learning process.

Finally, remember to recognize and celebrate progress. Knowing the benefits of formative assessment for students and their teachers makes it difficult to be patient and accept small victories. Sometimes it is easy to misinterpret slow progress or incremental change as resistance. Look for evidence of formative assessment and celebrate it everywhere that you see it—each small step and daily triumph. Mutual encouragement and shared pride can go a long way.

What Are Specific Strategies That Can Help School Leaders Take Formative Assessment Schoolwide?

In Chapters 1 through 7 we suggested ways to use the elements of the formative assessment process to guide and encourage classroom teachers to put formative assessment to work in their individual classrooms. What follows are strategies that focus on beginning and sustaining school-level discussions. These strategies will promote goal-directed action plans for taking formative assessment schoolwide.

What we suggest focuses squarely on the role that teacher beliefs play in your school—individually and collectively. As we explained in Chapter 1, it is critical to quickly inoculate against the all too common misconception regarding formative assessment: *I am already doing this.* Remember, you are not trying to encourage teachers to "do" formative assessment; rather, you are asking teachers to collectively embrace an important conceptual change.

We begin by describing how to engage teachers individually and then collectively in taking the formative assessment pulse of their classrooms, and then we explain how to share information to set collective goals for the school.

Beginning with Sharing Learning Targets and Criteria for Success

The elements of the formative assessment process must work together with quality, consistency, and fidelity to have a positive effect on student achievement and motivation to learn. And although it is possible to take formative assessment schoolwide by beginning with any one of the elements, our continued work with administrators and schools convinces us that Shared Learning Targets and the Criteria for Success is the hub—the central element of the process (see Figure 8.1). And because of that, we suggest it as the first element to introduce and the element on which to focus.

This approach makes sense if you consider the three guiding questions of the formative assessment process: *Where am I going? Where am I now? What strategy or strategies can help me get to where I need to go?* The learning target is key. Without a clear understanding of where we are headed, the effects of the other elements decrease. For example, for feedback to truly feed forward it must be tightly tied to the learning targets. Even descriptive and timely feedback that suggests a learning strategy will have little effect if a shared learning target does not anchor that feedback. The same goes for student self-assessment; the learning target focuses the student's estimation of the gap between where the student is and where the student needs to be. In fact, understanding the learning target and using it as a North Star help students plot their course and monitor their progress. Students cannot set effective goals without knowing where they are headed. We can teach them how to ask questions, but unless they see inquiry as a way to make progress toward the learning target, their questions will do little to increase their understanding, confidence, and competence.

Just as important, shared learning targets drive instructional planning. The most innovative lesson plan will fall short if it does not intentionally help students

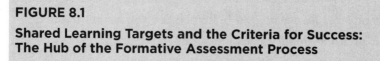

FIGURE 8.1

**Shared Learning Targets and the Criteria for Success:
The Hub of the Formative Assessment Process**

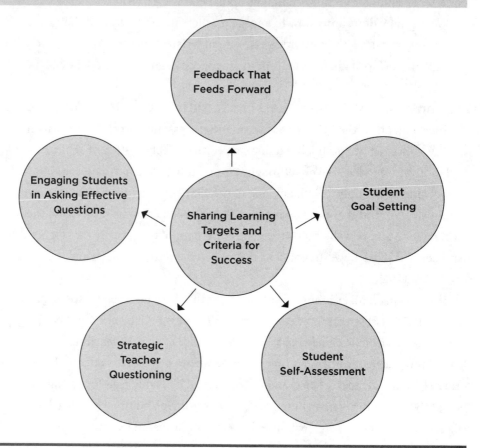

come to know and understand the important concepts and skills that make up the learning target. In the same vein, teacher questions are not strategic if those questions do not focus student attention on critical aspects of the concepts and skills essential to mastery of the learning target.

Finally, shared learning targets are imperative for educational leaders who intend to take formative assessment schoolwide. Teachers need to know where they are going. They need the time to examine those shared targets so that they can assess the gap between where they are and where they need to be in order to create strategies for getting there.

For these reasons and many more, shared learning targets that are clear, specific, and tied to exemplars of excellence increase the probability for success for educators and their students. The old adage holds true: if you do not know where you are headed, any road will take you there. A unified, strategic plan for taking formative assessment schoolwide begins with and is sustained by clearly communicated targets and criteria for success.

Taking the Formative Assessment Pulse of the Classroom

Humans often approach a new process like formative assessment with a delusion of familiarity. And so as we have said before, you can expect teachers, being all too human, to assume that they are already implementing formative assessment. In our work with teachers who are grappling with the formative assessment process, we often hear statements like this: "We already do this; we just call it something else."

Without a clear understanding of what it takes to implement all of the elements of the formative assessment process in the day-to-day and minute-by-minute work of the classroom, it is common for teachers to assume that they are already "doing" formative assessment at the highest levels of quality and consistency. That is why we suggest systematic and intentional inquiry into their classroom assessment practices as a good place to begin and as an honest reality check.

To help teachers assess their current practices, help them take the Formative Assessment Pulse of their classroom. Encourage them to reflect on three actual assessment experiences in their individual classrooms, on three separate days, using a format like the one in Figure 8.2. Encourage teachers to be as honest as possible as they document their assessment practices.

From the outset, work hard to establish an atmosphere of trust and sharing as you explain what you are asking teachers to do by asking them to take the Formative Assessment Pulse of their classrooms. Make sure to convey that teachers are gathering this evidence about their assessment practices to inform their own professional growth and focus their reflection. Remember that revealing what happens in one's classrooms can constitute a risk for many teachers and make some teachers very uncomfortable. Explain that your goal is not to judge

---

FIGURE 8.2

Checklist for Taking a Formative Assessment Pulse

Formative Assessment Pulse Point (1, 2, 3)   Date_____

Description of the Assessment (When did it take place, what was the format, timing, time limit, etc.):

Skills/Content That You Assessed:

Type of Assessment	**Uses of the Assessment (Check All That Apply)**		**My Purpose for the Assessment**
__ Written __ Oral __ Private conference __ Project __ Portfolio __ Essay __ Cooperative activity __ Presentation/ performance __ Other _____	**Formative** (*for* **Learning**) __ My students and I entered into the assessment with the intention to learn more about where we are, where we are headed, and how we are going to get there. __ My students and I used it to monitor excellence during the process of learning. __ My students and I used it for goal setting.	**Summative** (*of* **Learning**) __ I used it to evaluate overall student performance at the end of a unit of study or lesson. __ I used it to evaluate specific skills and/or knowledge at the end of a lesson or unit of study.	__ To analyze and direct lesson planning (content/process) __ To identify student needs __ To compare with other evidence of learning __ To contribute toward final grade __ To report to student/parent __ To help my students set goals
My Students' Role During the Assessment (Check All That Apply)			**Assessment Source**
__ Were aware of the skills and/or content to be assessed. __ Knew when they would be assessed. __ Helped develop the assessment. __ Identified specific strategies that they would use to succeed. __ Were aware of the criteria for success beyond what constituted a passing score. __ Had a rubric, checklist, or other way to monitor and regulate themselves during the assessment.			__ Textbook __ Teacher-made __ Another source (book, Web site, etc.) __ Teacher-modified or -refined (explain):

---

but to create a safe and open community of continuous inquiry and improvement to enhance student learning and achievement in your school. Describe how you will share information from the pulse points in professional conversations that are goal-directed, challenging, and yes, even unsettling, but necessary in order to work together to improve teaching and learning. Once teachers gather their three assessment pulse points, help them reflect on what the evidence shows about assessment practices in their classrooms and across the school.

Reflecting on the Three Assessment Pulse Points

Critical reflection that is honest, systematic, and intentional is vital for taking formative assessment schoolwide. Omit it at your own peril. Keep in mind that lasting change happens at a belief-altering level or not at all (Moss, 2002; Schreiber et al., 2007). Reflecting on the pulse points promotes cognitive dissonance by asking teachers to compare their actual assessment practices with highly effective formative assessment practices. This action will bring everyday assessment realities into sharp relief. The questions and prompts we suggest act as lenses that focus teacher reflection on specific criteria of high-quality formative assessment. Asking teachers to simply reflect on or assess what they do is not the kind of reflection that initiates change. General or shallow reflection does not produce crucial insights that illuminate the gap between what teachers actually do and what they need to do to gain skill and expertise in the formative assessment process.

Encourage teachers to focus their inquiry into their classroom assessment practices through the combined lenses of their three assessment pulse points. Then walk them through two phases of inquiry. Phase 1 asks teachers to recognize patterns in assessment practice, note specific areas of strength, and identify areas for growth. Phase 2 moves them from analyzing their practices to systematically and intentionally reflecting on the effect of their assessment patterns; it helps them to individually and collectively set goals and create action plans.

To begin, introduce teachers to the purpose and the questions that frame Phase 1 inquiry (see Figure 8.3). Notice that the first set of questions in Phase 1 deals with the assessment practices teachers used. Do their practices yield strong evidence of learning? If not, what are confounding variables or areas of assessment bias linked to their assessment practices? The second set of questions in Phase 1 prompts teachers to think in goal-directed ways about their formative assessment expertise. Once again, draw on the guiding questions of the formative assessment process to explain that Phase 1 inquiry will help teachers think deeply about their practices to gauge formative assessment in their classroom: *Where am I? Where am I going? What strategy or strategies can help me get to where I need to go?*

Phase 2 inquiry takes teacher reflection to a much deeper, belief-altering level. Teachers are confronted with strategic "action questions" (see Figure 8.4). Each action question is paired with an analytical rubric—a continuum—that asks teachers to compare their present level of practice with the specific criteria characterizing high-quality formative assessment.

As we suggest in our discussion of self-assessment in Chapter 5, make sure teachers have ample time to discuss the rubrics and actively process the criteria. This will help teachers have the criteria "in mind" so that the review of their work will be "mindful," specific, and focused on the relevant characteristics of high-quality formative assessment.

Use the action questions and formative assessment continuums to help teachers plot where they are, set goals, and identify strategies for increasing their professional expertise about the formative assessment process.

Collaborative Sharing and Action Planning

Once each teacher has created individual action steps, ask the teachers to share their action steps with each other. Sharing goals is an integral part of the professional accountability conversation that you want to begin and maintain. At first the sharing may be very straightforward and tenuous. As teachers come to believe that they are in this together, that this is not a choice but a collective endeavor, and that it is safe to share strengths and needs, the conversations will grow deeper and more productive.

Feel free to create your own strategic action questions, continuums of criteria, and prompts for action steps that reflect the unique characteristics of your school. Teachers can work together to create self-assessment rubrics for themselves to use as they continue to ramp up their expertise with formative assessment.

Use collaborative inquiry, reflection, self-assessment, and goal setting to embed and sustain formative assessment as a constant and continuous learning process rather than as isolated techniques or a one-time event. You can cultivate increased

FIGURE 8.3
Reflection Phase 1

Inquiry into My Assessment Design

Considering the actual practices documented in each assessment pulse point, . . .

- Did I truly assess the specific content or skill I intended?
- Did my students need content or skills other than those specified for the assessment in order to succeed?
- Did the assessment measure that content or those skills more than the content or skills that I intended to gauge?
- Did the assessment that I used in each instance fulfill the assessment purpose? Why or why not?

Inquiry into My Assessment Patterns

Considering the actual practices documented in the three assessment pulse points, I must conclude that I usually use classroom assessments to . . .

- Guide student learning.
- Assess the current status of each student's progress on specific skills/content.
- Plan and direct further instruction.
- Uncover gaps in my understanding and practice to guide my professional learning needs.
- Make decisions about the effectiveness of my teaching.
- Help my students with self-assessment and goal setting.
- Collect strong evidence of student learning.

competence in formative assessment by engaging teachers in professional conversations about learning and achievement.

A Final Thought

We purposely focused this book on six elements of the formative assessment process that work together to help students intentionally harness the workings of their own minds to increase their achievement and generate motivation to learn. We cannot state strongly enough that the primary goal of formative assessment

FIGURE 8.4
Reflection Phase 2

Action Question 1: Are my formative assessment efforts research-driven?

BEGINNING	PROGRESSING	EXEMPLARY

I am beginning to review research on the effect of formative assessment on teacher quality, student achievement, and motivation to learn.

I have a basic familiarity with research on the effect of formative assessment on teacher quality, student achievement, and motivation to learn.

I am very familiar with the research on the effect of formative assessment on teacher quality, student achievement, and motivation to learn. The intentional integration of this research is evident in my daily classroom practices.

I will take these action steps to increase my familiarity with the research on formative assessment:

Action Question 2: Do I intentionally collect and analyze information about my teaching and its effect on my students' learning?

BEGINNING	PROGRESSING	EXEMPLARY

I am eager to begin collecting evidence on the ways that my teaching affects student learning in my classroom.

Some of my lessons demonstrate my efforts to use formative assessment to refine and revise my teaching in ways that have a proven positive effect on student learning in my classroom.

I consistently use formative assessment to collect strong evidence of student learning and to raise the quality of my own teaching. I can document exactly which instructional practices have had positive effects on student learning in my classroom.

I will take these action steps to monitor the effect of my teaching on my students' learning and to raise the quality of my instruction:

FIGURE 8.4

Reflection Phase 2 *(cont.)*

Action Question 3: Do my students have opportunities in my classroom to assess and regulate their own learning?

BEGINNING	PROGRESSING	EXEMPLARY
My students are not aware that they can assess and regulate their own learning. I will take steps to raise their self-assessment awareness and skill.	My students have basic self-assessment knowledge and skill. They usually have a general idea of what they must do more of or less of, or what they should do next to be successful. I am not consistent in making self-assessment an integral part of each lesson.	My students and I are partners in learning. We consistently share information about learning goals and success criteria. My students are skilled self-assessors and confident self-regulated learners.

I will take these action steps to share more information with my students about where they are, where they need to go, and what they should do to get there:

Action Question 4: Do I use the formative assessment process as I am teaching to guide what I do?

BEGINNING	PROGRESSING	EXEMPLARY
I collect information on student learning at the end of a lesson, not while I am teaching. I use evidence of student learning to improve how I will teach the lesson to the next group of students.	I am sometimes able to guide my teaching based on information that I am gathering. I always use what I know about my students' learning to reteach concepts until they reach mastery.	I know exactly where my students and I are headed and the criteria for success. I constantly gauge student learning to monitor and adjust my teaching as I am working with my students.

I will take these action steps to gauge student understanding while I am teaching:

FIGURE 8.4
Reflection Phase 2 *(cont.)*

Action Question 5: Do I draw on formative assessment information to guide my conversations with parents, other teachers, and administrators about student learning and achievement in my classroom?

BEGINNING　　　　　PROGRESSING　　　　　EXEMPLARY

I rely mostly on assessment of learning, and the information that I collect exists as grades and scores. What I collect does little to help me describe the learning that is and is not taking place in a way that is helpful to others.	I use the formative assessment process to gather information to share with others about student learning in my classroom. This evidence provides a rich description of where my students are in relation to my learning goals.	I consistently collect precise, timely, and descriptive evidence from the formative assessment process that guides my conversations with others regarding exactly what my students know and are able to do as they make progress toward my clearly defined learning targets.

I will take these action steps to move beyond using grades and scores to talk with others about student learning in my classroom:

---

is to improve student learning. Although the benefits for professional growth are significant, that professional growth must increase student achievement. And though we shared practical strategies for teachers and school leaders throughout the book, we caution again that implementing the strategies as disjointed techniques will not produce high-quality formative learning experiences that have a positive effect on student achievement. Optimal learning environments flourish in schools where formative assessment is not just what educators "do" but is an indicator of what educators believe in and value.

We sincerely hope this book encourages school leaders to consider that learning—and, most crucially, learning how to learn—is the key to increased achievement for *all* students. So in a very real way, we wrote this book to support school leaders who have the courage and the commitment to move from viewing themselves as instructional leaders to seeing themselves as the leading learners in their schools.

We firmly believe what Theodore Roosevelt proposed years ago: "Far and away the best prize that life offers is the chance to work hard at work worth doing." Leading schools is hard work—we don't need to tell you that. But, as we have witnessed in our own teaching and in schools where we are honored to work beside so many dedicated professionals, teaching students how to learn, instead of merely what to learn, is valuable work that is well worth doing.

References

Alvermann, D., Young, J., Weaver, D., Hinchman, K., Moore, D., & Phelps, S. (1996). Middle school and high school students' perceptions of how they experience text-based discussions: A multicase study. *Reading Research Quarterly, 31*(3), 244–267.

Ames, C. (1992). Classrooms: Goals, structures, and student motivation. *Journal of Educational Psychology, 84*(3), 261–271.

Andrade, H. L., Du, Y., & Wang, X. (2008). Putting rubrics to the test: The effect of a model, criteria generation, and rubric-referenced self-assessment on elementary school students' writing. *Educational Measurement: Issues and Practice, 27*(2), 3–13.

Bandura, A. (1997). *Self-efficacy: The exercise of control.* New York: W. H. Freeman.

Bandura, A., & Cervone, D. (1986). Differential engagement of self-reactive influences in cognitive motivation. *Organizational Behavior and Human Decision Process, 38,* 92–113.

Bangert-Drowns, R. L., Kulik, C. C., Kulik, J. A., & Morgan, M. (1991). The instructional effect of feedback in test-like events. *Review of Educational Research, 61,* 213–238.

Barell, J. (2003). *Developing more curious minds.* Alexandria, VA: ASCD.

Bereiter, C., & Scardamalia, M. (1989). Intentional learning as a goal of instruction. In L. B. Resnick (Ed.), *Knowing, learning, and instruction: Essays in honor of Robert Glaser* (pp. 361–392). Hillsdale, NJ: Lawrence Erlbaum Associates.

Black, P., Harrison, C., Lee, C., Marshall, B., & Wiliam, D. (2003). *Assessment for learning: Putting it into practice.* Maidenhead, Berkshire, UK: Open University Press.

Black, P., & Wiliam, D. (1998). Inside the black box: Raising standards through classroom assessment. *Phi Delta Kappan, 80*(2), 139–148.

Boston, C. (2002). *The concept of formative assessment.* College Park, MD: ERIC Clearinghouse on Assessment and Evaluation. (ERIC Document Reproduction Service No. ED470206, 2002-10-00). Available: http://www.vtaide.com/png/ERIC/Formative-Assessment.htm

Bransford, J. D., Brown, A. L., & Cocking, R. R. (Eds.). (2000). *How people learn: Brain, mind, experience, and school.* Washington, DC: National Academy Press.

Brookhart, S. M. (2006). *Formative assessment strategies for every classroom: An ASCD action tool.* Alexandria, VA: ASCD.

Brookhart, S. M. (2008). *How to give effective feedback to your students.* Alexandria, VA: ASCD.

Brookhart, S. M., Andolina, M., Zuza, M., & Furman, R. (2004). Minute math: An action research study of student self-assessment. *Educational Studies in Mathematics, 57,* 213–227.

Butler, D. L., & Winne, P. H. (1995). Feedback and self-regulated learning: A theoretical synthesis. *Review of Educational Research, 65,* 245–281.

Cazden, C. (2001). *Classroom discourse: The language of teaching and learning.* Portsmouth, NH: Heinemann.

Chappuis, J. (2005). Helping students understand assessment. *Educational Leadership, 63*(3), 39–43.

Clarke, S. (2005). *Formative assessment in the secondary classroom.* London: Hodder Murray.

Darling-Hammond, L. (1999). *Teacher quality and student achievement: A review of state policy evidence.* Seattle, WA: Center for the Study of Teaching and Policy, University of Washington.

Deci, E. L., Koestner, R., & Ryan, R. M. (1999). A meta-analytic review of experiments examining the effects of extrinsic rewards on intrinsic motivation. *Psychological Bulletin, 125,* 627–668.

Dillon, J. T. (1984). Research on questioning and discussion. *Educational Leadership, 42*(3), 50–56.

Dillon, J. T. (1988). *Questioning and teaching: A manual of practice.* New York: Teachers College Press.

Downey, C. J., Steffy, B. E., English, F. W., Frase, L. E., & Poston, W. K. (2004). *The three-minute classroom walk-though: Changing school supervisory practice one teacher at a time.* Thousand Oaks, CA: Corwin Press.

Elmore, R. (2000). *Building a new structure for school leadership.* Washington, DC: Albert Shanker Institute.

Elmore, R. F. (2004). *School reform from the inside out: Policy, practice, and performance.* Cambridge, MA: Harvard Education Press.

Fisher, D., & Frey, N. (2007). *Checking for understanding: Formative assessment techniques for your classroom.* Alexandria, VA: ASCD.

Furtak, E. M., Ruiz-Primo, M. A., Shemwell, J. T., Ayala, C. C., Brandon, P. R., Shavelson, R. J., & Yin, Y. (2008). On the fidelity of implementing embedded formative assessments and its relation to student learning. *Applied Measurement in Education, 21*(4), 360–389.

Glickman, C. D., Gordon, S. P., & Ross-Gordon, J. M. (1998). *Supervision of instruction: A developmental approach* (4th ed.). Needham Heights, MA: Allyn and Bacon.

Gronlund, N. R., & Brookhart, S. M. (2009). *Gronlund's writing instructional objectives* (8th ed.). Upper Saddle River, NJ: Merrill/Prentice-Hall.

Hale, M. S., & City, E. A. (2006). *Leading student-centered discussions: Talking about texts in the classroom.* Thousand Oaks, CA: Corwin Press.

Hall, G., & Hord, S. (2000). *Implementing change: Patterns, principles, and potholes.* Boston: Allyn and Bacon.

Hanushek, E. A., Kain, J. F., O'Brien, D. M., & Rivkin, S. G. (2005). *The market for teacher quality.* (NBER Working Paper 11154). Washington, DC: National Bureau of Economic Research.

Hastings, S. (2003). *Questions.* The TES. Market Harborough, Wales: TSL Education LTD.

Hattie, J., & Timperley, H. (2007). The power of feedback. *Review of Educational Research, 77,* 81–112.

Higgins, K. M., Harris, N. A., & Kuehn, L. L. (1994). Placing assessment into the hands of young children: A study of self-generated criteria and self-assessment. *Educational Assessment, 2,* 309–324.

Hunkins, F. P. (1995). *Teaching thinking through effective questioning.* Norwood, MA: Christopher-Gordon.

Kluger, A. N., & DeNisi, A. (1996). The effects of feedback interventions on performance: A historical review, a meta-analysis, and a preliminary feedback intervention theory. *Psychological Bulletin, 119,* 254–284.

Kulhavy, R. W. (1977). Feedback in written instruction. *Review of Educational Research, 47*(2), 211–232.

Locke, E. A. (2002). Setting goals for life and happiness. In C. R. Snyder & S. J. Lopez (Eds.), *Handbook for positive psychology* (pp. 299–312). New York: Oxford University Press.

Locke, E. A., & Latham, G. P. (1990). *A theory of goal-setting and task performance.* Englewood Cliffs, NJ: Prentice-Hall.

Locke, E. A., & Latham, G. P. (2002). Building a practically useful theory of goal setting and task performance. *American Psychologist, 57,* 705–717.

Michaels, S., O'Conner, M. C., & Hall, M. W., with Resnick, L. B. (2002). *Accountable talk: Classroom conversation that works.* [3 CD-ROM set]. Pittsburgh, PA: University of Pittsburgh.

Morgan, N., & Saxton, J. (1991). *Teaching, questioning, and learning.* London: Routledge.

Moss, C. M. (2000). Teaching as intentional learning: Examining our assumptions. *Network Newsnotes,* International Network of Principals' Centers. Cambridge, MA: Harvard Graduate School of Education.

Moss, C. M. (2001). *Teaching as intentional learning: A resource guide for the teacher scholar.* Pittsburgh, PA: Duquesne University School of Education.

Moss, C. M. (2002). Professional learning on the cyber sea: What is the point of contact? In R. Hall (Ed.), Special Topic Issue: World Wide Web and Education, *Journal of CyberPsychology and Behavior, 1*(3), 41–50.

Moss, C., & McCown, R. R. (2007, February). *Toward a theory of signature pedagogy: The case of (and for) systematic and intentional inquiry.* Paper presented at the annual meeting of the American Association of Colleges for Teacher Education, New York.

National Education Association. (2003). *Balanced assessment: The key to accountability and improved student learning.* Washington, DC: Author.

Newman, R. S., & Goldin, L. (1990). Children's reluctance to seek help with schoolwork. *Journal of Educational Psychology, 82*(1), 92–100.

Pajares, F. (1996). Self-efficacy beliefs in academic settings. *Review of Educational Research, 66*(4), 543–578.

Perkins, D. (1992). *Smart schools: Better thinking and learning for every child.* New York: Free Press.

Perkins, D. (1995). *Outsmarting IQ: The emerging science of learnable intelligence.* New York: Free Press.

Pintrich, P. R., & Schunk, D. H. (2002). *Motivation in education: Theory, research, and applications* (2nd ed.). Upper Saddle River, NJ: Merrill/Prentice-Hall.

Popham, W. J. (2008). *Transformative assessment.* Alexandria, VA: ASCD.

Robinson, F. P. (1941). *Diagnostic and remedial techniques for effective study.* New York: Harper Brothers.

Rop, C. F. (2002). The meaning of student inquiry questions: A teacher's beliefs and responses. *International Journal of Science Education, 24*(7), 717–736.

Ross, J. A., Hogaboam-Gray, A., & Rolheiser, C. (2002). Student self-evaluation in grade 5–6 mathematics: Effects on problem-solving achievement. *Educational Assessment, 8*(1), 3–58.

Rowe, M. B. (1974). Relation of wait-time and rewards to the development of language, logic, and fate control. *Journal of Research in Science Teaching, 11*(4), 292.

Rowe, M. B. (1986, January–February). Wait time: Slowing down may be a way of speeding up! *Journal of Teacher Education, 37*(1), 43–50.

Rowe, M. B. (2003). Wait-time and rewards as instructional variables, their influence on language, logic and fate control: Part one—Wait-time. *Journal of Research in Science Teaching, #40 Supplement,* S19–32.

Ryan, R. M., & Deci, E. L. (2000). Self-determination theory and the facilitation of intrinsic motivation, social development, and well-being. *American Psychologist, 55*(1), 68–78.

Sadler, P. M., & Good, E. (2006). The impact of self- and peer-grading on student learning. *Educational Assessment, 11*(1), 1–31.

Sato, M., & Atkin, J. M. (2006/2007). Supporting change in classroom assessment. *Educational Leadership, 64*(4), 76–79.

Schreiber, J. B., Moss, C. M., & Staab, J. (2007). A preliminary examining of a theoretical model for researching educator beliefs. *Semiotica, 164,* 153–172.

Shavelson, R. J., Young, D. B., Ayala, C. C., Brandon, P. R., Furtak, E. M., Ruiz-Primo, M. A., Tomita, J. K., & Yin, Y. (2008). On the impact of curriculum-embedded formative assessment on learning: A collaboration between curriculum and assessment developers. *Applied Measurement in Education, 21*(4), 295–314.

Spiegel, D. L. (2005). *Classroom discussion.* New York: Scholastic Inc.

Stahl, R. J. (1994). *Using "think-time" and "wait-time" skillfully in the classroom* (ERIC Digest). Bloomington, IN: ERIC Clearinghouse for Social Studies and Social Science Education. (ERIC Document Reproduction Service No. ED370885).

Stipek, D. J. (2002). *Motivation to learn: Integrating theory and practice* (4th ed.). Boston: Allyn & Bacon.

Thompson, M., & Wiliam, D. (2007). *Tight but loose: A conceptual framework for scaling up school reform.* Paper presented at the annual meeting of the American Educational Research Association, Chicago, Illinois.

Tobin, K. (1987). The role of wait time in higher cognitive level learning. *Review of Educational Research, 57,* 69–95.

Vispoel, W. P., & Austin, J. R. (1995). Success and failure in junior high school: A critical incident approach to understanding students' attributional beliefs. *American Educational Research Journal, 32*(2), 377–412.

Walsh, J. A., & Sattes, B. D. (2005). *Quality questioning: Research-based practice to engage every learner.* Thousand Oaks, CA: Corwin Press.

Wells, G. (2001). The case for dialogic inquiry. In G. Wells (Ed.), *Action, talk and text: Learning and teaching through inquiry* (pp. 171–194). New York: Teachers College Press.

Yin, Y., Shavelson, R. J., Ayala, C. C., Ruiz-Primo, M. A., Brandon, P. R., Furtak, E. M., Tomita, J. K., & Young, D. B. (2008). On the impact of formative assessment on student motivation, achievement, and conceptual change. *Applied Measurement in Education, 21*(4), 335–359.

Zimmerman, B. (1998). Academic studying and the development of personal skill: A self-regulatory perspective. *Educational Psychologist, 33*(2/3), 73–86.

Zimmerman, B. J. (2001). Theories of self-regulated learning and academic achievement: An overview and analysis. In B. J. Zimmerman & H. D. Shunk (Eds.), *Self-regulated learning and academic achievement: Theoretical perspectives* (pp. 1–37). Mahwah, NJ: Lawrence Erlbaum Associates.

INDEX

ABOUT THE AUTHORS

Connie M. Moss, EdD, is an Associate Professor in the Department of Educational Foundations and Leadership in the School of Education at Duquesne University and Director of the Center for Advancing the Study of Teaching and Learning. She served for 25 years as a K–12 educator, spending 17 of those years in early childhood, elementary, and middle school classrooms. She continued her public school service as an educational leader of multidistrict, regional, and statewide support initiatives in curriculum planning and assessment, early childhood, and instructional support. She has been an invited speaker and presenter in over 600 school districts, 100 universities and colleges, and numerous educational associations and organizations. Her publications and presentations examine the role beliefs play in intentional learning, effective teaching, formative assessment, and educational leadership for social justice. She can be reached at moss@castl.duq.edu.

Susan M. Brookhart, PhD, is an independent educational consultant based in Helena, Montana. She works with ASCD as an ASCD Faculty Member, providing on-site professional development in formative assessment. She has taught both elementary and middle school. She was a Professor in and Chair of the Department of Educational Foundations and Leadership at Duquesne University, where she currently serves as Senior Research Associate in the Center for Advancing the Study of Teaching and Learning in the School of Education. She serves on the state assessment advisory committee for the state of Montana. She has been the Education columnist for *National Forum,* the journal of Phi Kappa Phi, and Editor of *Educational Measurement: Issues and Practice,* a journal of the National Council on Measurement in Education. She is the author or coauthor of several books, including ASCD's *How to Give Effective Feedback to Your Students.* She can be reached at susanbrookhart@bresnan.net.

Related ASCD Resources: Formative Assessment

At the time of publication, the following ASCD resources were available (ASCD stock numbers appear in parentheses). For up-to-date information about ASCD resources, go to www.ascd.org.

Multimedia

Formative Assessment Strategies for Every Classroom: An ASCD Action Tool by Susan M. Brookhart (#707010)

Guide for Instructional Leaders, Guide 2: An ASCD Action Tool by Grant Wiggins, John L. Brown, and Ken O'Connor (#703105)

Networks

Visit the ASCD Web site (www.ascd.org) and click on About ASCD. Go to the section on Networks for information about professional educators who have formed groups around topics such as "Assessment for Learning." Look in the Network Directory for current facilitators' addresses and phone numbers.

Online Courses

Visit the ASCD Web site (www.ascd.org) for the following professional development opportunities:
Designing Performance Assessments (#PD02OC22)
Exemplary Assessment: Measurement That's Useful (#PD03OC33)

Print Products

Checking for Understanding: Formative Assessment Techniques for Your Classroom by Douglas Fisher and Nancy Frey (#107023)

Classroom Assessment and Grading That Work by Robert J. Marzano (#106006)

Improving Student Learning One Teacher at a Time by Jane Pollock (#107005)

Educational Leadership, December 2007/January 2008: Informative Assessment (#108023)

Enhancing Professional Practice: A Framework for Teaching by Charlotte Danielson (#106034)

Exploring Formative Assessment (The Professional Learning Community Series) by Susan Brookhart (#109038)

How to Give Effective Feedback to Your Students by Susan M. Brookhart (#108019)

Instruction That Measures Up: Successful Teaching in the Age of Accountability by W. James Popham (#108048)

Making Standards Useful in the Classroom by Robert J. Marzano and Mark W. Haystead (#108006)

Transformative Assessment by W. James Popham (#108018)

Video and DVD

Formative Assessment in Content Areas Series (Three DVDs, each with a professional development program) (#609034)

Giving Effective Feedback to Your Students DVD Series (Three DVDs, each with a professional development program) (#609035)

The Power of Formative Assessment to Advance Learning (Three DVDs with a comprehensive user guide) (#608066)

THE WHOLE CHILD The Whole Child Initiative helps schools and communities create learning environments that allow students to be healthy, safe, engaged, supported, and challenged. To learn more about other books and resources that relate to the whole child, visit www.wholechildeducation.org.

For more information, visit us on the World Wide Web (http://www.ascd.org); send an e-mail message to member@ascd.org; call the ASCD Service Center (1-800-933-ASCD or 703-578-9600, then press 2); send a fax to 703-575-5400; or write to Information Services, ASCD, 1703 N. Beauregard St., Alexandria, VA 22311-1714 USA.